HydroRobics®

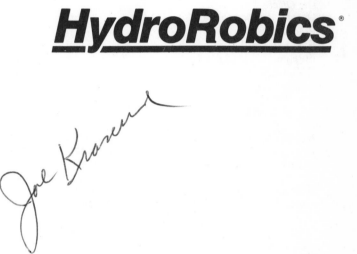

Published by Leisure Press
A division of Human Kinetics Publishers, Inc.
Box 5076, Champaign, IL 61825-5076
1-800-747-4457

UK Office:
Human Kinetics Publishers (UK) Ltd.
PO Box 18
Rawdon, Leeds LS19 6TG
England
(0532) 504211

10 9 8 7 6 5

ISBN 0-88011-266-2

Cover design: Debbie Silverman
Cover photograph: Jeff Whalen
Text cartoons: Mike Swaim
Text illustrations: Koula Iliopoulos

HydroRobics®

A water exercise program
for individuals of all ages
and fitness levels.

2nd EDITION

Joseph A. Krasevec
Diane C. Grimes

Leisure Press
Champaign, Illinois

DEDICATION

To
Jeff who made us work
and
Jodie who made us play

CONTENTS

FOREWORD

The practical ideas described here that now benefit only a few could, if used widely, enhance the lives of many. This book provides information that can be understood and utilized by a wide range of readers. Its procedures have been tested and found to be helpful in improving and maintaining personal fitness.

Many books have been written about the importance of, and need for, physical and emotional fitness. The gap between knowing and doing is narrowed and crossed when information is clearly presented and action is motivated by measured progress. This book is written to inform, explain and guide each reader toward improved fitness and personal satisfaction.

Water activity has been used in many agencies for the benefit of individuals and groups. A wide variety of methods and programs have been developed and found to be satisfactory. It is well for each individual to select and use regularly the program best suited to her or his individual interests and needs. This book can be the basis for launching a practical personalized exercise program of lasting value.

One of the authors, Joseph A. Krasevec, has been a professional colleague for a dozen years and an associate in the work of the USOC Education Council since 1973. His work on the faculties of two large universities has made substantial contributions to students as well as to members of the community at large. His experience and that of his co-author, Diane Grimes, make this book, with its excellent illustrations, a personal reference that will continue to motivate you as you strive toward a goal of physical fitness.

HAROLD T. FRIERMOOD, Ed. D.[*]

[*]
National Director, YMCA Health, Physical Education and Sports, (1943–1968)
Former Executive Director, Council for National Cooperation in Aquatics (1968–1975)
Member, U.S. Olympic Committee (1944–present)
Chairman, U.S. Olympic Committee's Education Council (1971–1984)

PREFACE

If you have never been an athlete or even a weekend sports enthusiast, you've probably also managed to avoid regular physical exercise. What this means is that you're probably not physically fit!

Most non-athletes associate exercise with hard work, stiff and sore muscles, perspiration and dubious results. None of these thoughts makes it easier to begin any sort of exercise program, but we have a pleasant surprise for those of you who want to be fit and dread what it takes to get there. HYDROROBICS is an exercise program that does not fit the traditional exercise "mold." It's easy to learn, appropriate for people at all fitness levels, is done in the water comfort of a swimming pool (no sweat!), does not result in soreness, and tones the muscles of all parts of the body! If you're the kind of person who isn't easily convinced, especially about doing things that you expect will be unpleasant, you're probably wondering why you haven't heard about this "miracle" program before. Students at universities, YMCAs and other organized groups with access to swimming pools have been doing water exercises for years. Persons with physical handicaps have also used water as a combination therapy and exercise medium. But written material about HYDROROBICS has usually been geared toward class/group learning, not toward an individual learning independently, from clear explanations and diagrams, and then adapting a program that is right for their own fitness levels.

This book hopes to do just that. It also hopes to lead you to the excitement and good feelings that go with HYDROROBICS. One of the authors of this book is an athlete and a university instructor of HYDROROBICS; the co-author is a non-athlete who has become an enthusiastic practitioner, promoter and occasional teacher of HYDROROBICS. We hope that our experience and enthusiasm will lead you to an approach toward physical fitness that you can both make a regular part of your life—and enjoy!

The Authors

_____
_____
_____
_____
_____
_____
_____

ACKNOWLEDGMENTS

Koula Iliopoulos, artist
Mike Swaim, cartoonist
Jeff Whalen, front cover photographer
Atlanta Downtown Marriott, cover photo location
Bob Khoury, Showcase Photographic Equipment, cameras
Linda Lord, Kathy Karanungan, typists
Amanda Tarkington, proofreader
Students of our HYDROROBICS classes, Georgia State University, and especially Judith Rice for her suggestions, encouragement, and dedication to HYDROROBICS

PART ONE

GETTING STARTED

1

EXERCISE: WHAT'S IN IT FOR ME?

Exercise. Why is everyone making such a big deal about exercise? You're bombarded with magazine articles on diet and physical fitness and programs on radio and television. Jane Fonda and Richard Simmons have captured national attention by promoting physical activity as an essential ingredient in the maintenance of good health. Even your neighbors have donned running shoes, and you go out of your way to avoid them because you can't handle another lecture on the value of exercise.

Physical Fitness Comes in Vogue

Well, you might as well get used to the concept of exercising, because America is turned on to it. Ever since the health of the nation was given bad marks by the Surgeon General back in the 1950's and 1960's, a major shift in attitude toward exercise has emerged among the American people. In 1956 former president Dwight D. Eisenhower responded to the growing need of educating the American public by creating what is now called The President's Council on Physical Fitness and Sports (PCPFS). One of its first attempts to unfold the mysteries of exercise was to distribute a monthly national newsletter on physical fitness and sports. It also began acting as a central coordinating agency for the many national governmental agencies involved in promoting physical fitness and sports activities.

Another major contribution was made by former president John F. Kennedy, who helped accelerate the nation's interest in physical fitness and sports with his youthful and physically active image during his term of office. Frequent mention of physical fitness in his speeches and his personal sports participation with his family captured the attention of the media and in turn established him as a role model for many Americans.

Finally, one of the major physical fitness movements in this country was initiated by Dr. Kenneth Cooper, when he introduced his book, *Aerobics*, in the early 1960's. The book explained in simple language the meaning and importance of cardiorespiratory fitness, one of the major components of physical fitness. Today, Dr. Kenneth Cooper is often referred to as the "father of modern physical fitness."

These are only a few of the significant contributions responsible for generating a national interest in physical exercise and sports.

Now we are in the 1980's, and every indication is that Americans have begun to accept the need to incorporate some form of physical activity into their everyday lives. A recent national survey entitled, "The Perrier Study: Fitness in America" (1979) conducted by Louis Harris and Associates, is positive proof that physical activity has taken root among the American public. One of their findings indicated that approximately 59% of the public engages in some form of physical activity. Physical fitness has taken on a national image. We hope that you become part of that image.

Health Defined

"Physical fitness" and "health" are often used interchangeably. Because of this, it is important that we understand their relationship to one another. The World Health Organization (WHO) describes health as "a state of complete physical, mental, and social well-being and not merely the absence of disease and infirmity." This means you should not automatically think you are fit just because nothing is wrong with you medically. Neither should you declare yourself in excellent health just because you have high levels of physical fitness. You must develop habits that will develop both physical fitness and health. Physical fitness plays a supporting role in the total health concept, but you still need to develop good eating habits by selecting highly nutritious foods, get enough sleep, and control the stress factors which are constantly knocking on our doors.

You should ingrain habits that will develop both physical fitness and health.

You're in Charge of Your Health

By now you probably suspect that exercise may offer something of value. Well, you're right. Good health! And we know everyone likes to enjoy good health. You may have heard or read about the nation's leading causes of death. In order of incidence they are: heart disease, cancer, stroke and accident. Unfortunately, if you're like most people, you probably don't let these facts bother you, because you have the attitude, "Oh, it will never happen to me." But if you know that one American dies every 60 seconds from heart attack, you might begin to think a little differently.

The important point to make is that *you* are in control of your destiny. It is the wise and unwise decisions you make which positively or negatively affect your health. It is the responsibility of all Americans to arrange their lifestyles in a way that can provide the best guarantees for good health.

Preventive Medicine Is the Answer

One thing you can do *now* to help maintain a healthy life is to initiate preventive measures. Mr. Walter B. Gerkin, a chairman and chief executive officer of the Pacific Mutual Insurance Company, agrees. In a national survey on the health status of Americans, he said that Americans are going to have to give more attention to health maintenance if they are to have healthier, happier, and more productive lives. He was specifically quoted as saying, "A major shift from curative to preventive medicine, clearly, is one whose time has come."

It's ironic when you consider that the health insurance industry in the United States, a leading nation of health care advances, rewards its policy holders by paying insurance claims only when they are sick and/or require an operation. While it may be outdated, the ancient Chinese had a point: They only paid their physicians for keeping them healthy. Once ill, they stopped payment.

Preventive   medicine is not new to the American public. Millions of dollars are made each year by companies and individuals who advertise such claims as "lose 20 pounds in one week," or "develop a shapely figure in ten days," or "eat XYZ brand food and you'll be granted a disease-free life." The success of these gimmicks is evidence that the public wants to improve its health. Further consider how the multi-billion dollar vitamin and health food industry has the public trained to want a supplement to daily health from vitamins and health foods.

While there is much doubt as to the value of many of these claims and gimmicks, one thing is for sure—physical fitness as a means of improving health is gaining more and more support by the medical community. Research is being identified every day, validating this theory.

Physical Fitness Defined

Now that you have physical fitness and health in perspective, it is important to fully understand the nature of physical fitness. One thing is certain, physical fitness means different things to different people. For this reason we have chosen to present a standard definition of physical fitness for use in this book. The definition selected was published by H. Harrison Clarke of the University of Oregon and was eventually endorsed by PCPFS. With slight modification it was also approved by the American Academy of Physical Education. A portion of the definition follows:

> *Physical fitness is the ability to carry out everyday tasks with vigor and alertness, without undue fatigue, and with ample energy to engage in leisure time pursuits, and to meet the above average physical stresses encountered in emergency situations.*

Physical fitness is also explained as the capability of the heart muscle, lungs, and general muscle structure to operate at maximal efficiency. If you develop optimal efficiency, you improve the quality of health so that you can "get the best" enjoyment out of participation in your daily routine and recreational and athletic activities.

Physical Fitness Components

Physical fitness is made up of several physiological, health-related components which are positively affected by exercise. The components are cardiorespiratory endurance, flexibility, strength, muscular endurance and body composition. These components are not to be thought of as separate parts of the human system because they are totally interrelated and are at times dependent on each other.

Too often we confuse *health*-related components of physical fitness with *skill*-related components. The skill-related components most often mentioned are agility, balance, coordination, power, reaction time and speed. You would be primarily interested in skill-related components if you were concerned with improving your athletic performance.

Whether your reason for starting an exercise program is to improve your health or to improve your sports performance, you should develop a training program aimed at improving your *total* physical fitness—that means including all the components of physical fitness.

Let's take a more detailed look at the various components so that we may better understand their value in the overall scheme of developing physical fitness.

Cardiorespiratory (C-R) Endurance

Of all the components, this is the most important! Let's face it, your heart is the most important muscle in your body. Without a functioning heart, you die. Your life depends on the ability of the heart and circulatory system to transport much needed oxygen and nutrients to the working muscles as well as to remove wastes. The largest amount of work that can be performed by the muscles is limited by the capability of the cardiorespiratory system to deliver the necessary amounts of oxygen to the muscle. The largest amount of oxygen you can process in one minute is called your maximal oxygen uptake and is often referred to as your aerobic capacity. If the amount of work being performed exceeds your aerobic capacity, your muscles fatigue.

Cardiorespiratory endurance is developed by subjecting the heart and lung muscles to the overload principle. This means that you must place the C-R system under repeatedly greater workload than normal until it has adapted to the increased demand. You should also know that the rate of improvement is directly proportional to the amount of overload.

Overloading the C-R system is generally done by engaging in endurance or aerobic type activities such as bicycling, jogging, rapid walking, swimming, or HYDROROBICS, etc. The level of intensity, frequency, and duration of these activities is important if you are to achieve positive results. These items will be discussed in the chapter, "Designing your Personalized Program."

One way of gauging whether or not your overload is sufficient is to utilize the training pulse rate method. Exercise science research has provided us with the guideline that when performing C-R endurance type training, you must raise your pulse rate to at least 60-85% of your maximal attainable heart rate. Your maximal attainable heart rate is defined as the highest pulse rate you can achieve in a strenuous activity before you fatigue.

If you are just beginning an aerobic exercise program you should set your target pulse rate at 60%. As you improve your aerobic capacity, you can increase the target heart rate (training pulse rate) until you reach the desired training or exercise level. More on this later.

Muscular Strength

Muscular strength is of absolute importance to all human function and should not be compared to the rippling muscles of a body builder. It is defined as the ability to lift the maximum amount of weight at one time in a single repetition. If you lose strength, you will lose muscle tone and develop sagging and flabby muscles.

Loss of muscle tone coupled with a high body fat content will always lead to unwanted, unsightly bulges. This visible factor is what often makes us unhappy about our bodies.

Perhaps more importantly, if you lose strength you may not be able to perform well at everyday tasks in your profession, or in sports. It is also well known that if you have weak muscles, you will be more susceptible to injury. In addition, low back pain, a frequent complaint by many people is generally caused by weak abdominal muscles. In fact, approximately 80% of lower back problems are muscular in nature. With appropriate exercise you can, in most cases, remedy this common problem.

Therefore, the muscular strength component of physical fitness is one which should demand your attention. Proper strength development and maintenance greatly helps you develop a better self-concept. Also, consider the other benefits of proper strength maintenance—it aids proper alignment of bones (posture) and body organs, and helps prevent obesity because muscle activity burns calories.

Muscular strength, like cardiorespiratory endurance, is developed by applying the overload principle explained in the last section. This overload is obtained by engaging the muscles in resistance type exercises such as weight training. Three types of muscular training principles are used to develop strength. The first is isotonics. This method involves lifting a fixed weight through the full range of motion of the limb. Here the muscle contracts or shortens, causing what is called *dynamic* movement. Isometrics involves a *static* contraction of the muscle system in a fixed position which produces no movement. An example would be pressing your palms together or pushing against a wall or immoveable object. Isokinetics is a relatively new concept and combines both isotonics and isometrics. In effect, you move your body part through its full range of motion with a fixed weight and constant speed of movement.

Some weight training manufacturers like Nautilus and Paramount have designed a "variable resistance" factor into their equipment. This means that during the movement the weight application varies to accommodate the stronger and weaker angles of your muscles in the full range of movement.

Flexibility

Flexibility is the one component of physical fitness that deteriorates rapidly during the aging process. Flexibility is the ability to move a limb through its full range of motion at a joint or group of joints. Such characteristics as bending, stretching and twisting are commonly used to determine if you're flexible. Maintaining good flexibility and joint mobility will help you to prevent unnecessary muscle injury and soreness.

Flexibility is usually improved by doing calisthenics. *Static* stretching exercises are preferred and involve slow, sustained stretching of the muscles. To perform static stretches you should move the body parts slowly into the maximum stretch position. You'll know you are in a maximum stretch when you reach the point where you feel "comfortable pain." Experts suggest, once in this position, you stay there for at least 10 seconds or longer. Dynamic or ballistic (bouncing) stretching is not recommended for the beginner because it causes an abnormal stretch of the muscle. If your muscles are not trained or warmed up properly, you could seriously damage the muscles involved. Well conditioned athletes who are involved in sports requiring explosive movements would normally add ballistic type stretching exercises to their training program. You may add these types of stretching exercises once you are well into an exercise program and your muscles are adequately conditioned.

Muscular Endurance

Muscular endurance should not be confused with muscular strength. Muscular endurance is the ability of the muscle to exert a force repeatedly over a period of time. Many experts consider muscular endurance and cardiorespiratory endurance to be highly dependent on each other. Since the individual muscles of the body are dependent on the heart and lungs for oxygen and nutrients, muscular endurance is considered to be a prerequisite to cardiorespiratory endurance.

In order to develop muscular endurance the muscle must be subjected to an overload and moved repeatedly through the range of movement. The most traditional method of achieving endurance is by lifting free weights, i.e., in a weight training facility, according to a set routine. For example, if you want to develop your arm biceps you might lift a 20 or 30 pound weight (depending on current level of endurance) through the normal range of motion and do it ten times (this is called a "set"). Then you might repeat this set two or three times. This may get confusing when you consider that there is a variety of weight training equipment on the market (e.g., Nautilus,

Paramount, Universal), each with its own specific system of training principles. Regardless of the type of equipment used, the end results are usually the same—increased muscular endurance.

Body Composition

It has only been in recent years that body composition has been considered a component of physical fitness. It refers to the amount or percent of fat on your body as compared to lean body mass (muscle) and bone. Most people are particularly concerned about body composition because it has a lot to do with the way we look—that all-important figure!

While this is important, we must not forget that too much fat not only makes us look unshapely, but puts excess weight on our body. This excess weight adds unhealthy stress to our cardiorespiratory system and body joints. It interferes with our daily physical activity and increases risks of serious medical problems.

Obesity is usually caused by overconsumption of food and a sedentary lifestyle. If obesity is one of your problems, exercise may help you lose some of those unwanted pounds. People who are interested in a *healthy* approach to weight reduction or control should follow the advice of experts: decrease the amount of caloric intake (food consumption) and increase the amount of caloric expenditure (physical activity). If you're serious about controlling your weight, it will be helpful to know that the preferred average fat content for an adult male is 16-18% (of the body weight) and 18-22% for an adult female. More on this later.

Benefits of Exercise

You have just learned that physical fitness is made up of five major components. Can you name them without looking at the preceding section?

Developing each of these components to its fullest potential is considered to be a major benefit of exercise. In doing so, you will greatly improve the overall quality of your life. In addition to the major benefits, we would like to list a number of related benefits that you might look forward to *if you exercise.*

Exercise will help you to

- cope with stress
- have more energy
- improve your self image
- sleep better
- increase resistance to fatigue

- make new friends
- relax
- increase your work capacity
- decrease your chance for lower back problems
- improve your general appearance
- reduce injury to muscles
- improve sports performance
- delay the aging process
- control appetite
- control body weight
- prevent heart attack and cardiovascular disease

This list could go on . . . and on . . . and on . . . .

Well, are you convinced of the importance of exercise? If so, you can now understand why so many Americans engage in physical activity. If you are not already exercising, why don't you consider joining the national trend?

Whether you are just starting or are already exercising, why not consider starting a HYDROROBICS exercise program? Turn to the next chapter and learn more about this exciting and popular form of exercise in "HYDROROBICS Defined."

References

Corbin, Charles B.; Dowell, L. J.; Lindsey, R.; and Tolson, H. *Concepts in Physical Education*. Dubuque, Iowa: William C. Brown Company Publishers, 1981.

Getchell, Bud. *Physical Fitness—a Way of Life*. New York: John Wiley & Sons, 1983.

Louis Harris and Associates, Inc. *Health Maintenance*. Commissioned by Pacific Mutual Life Insurance Company, 1978.

The Committee on Exercise. *Exercise Testing and Training of Apparently Healthy Individuals: A Handbook for Physicians*. Dallas, Texas: American Heart Association, 1972.

Zohman, Lenore R. *Beyond Diet . . . Exercise Your Way to Fitness and Heart Health*. CPC International, Inc., 1974.

2

HYDROROBICS DEFINED

It is unlikely that you bought this book for its title. Most people who see the word HYDROROBICS for the first time are confused about its meaning. To some it sounds like a highly technical term from an engineering textbook. Both friends and students at Georgia State University, where "hydro" is a regular course offering, have kidded with us by saying the word sounds like a disease.

Hopefully some of you recognized the root word, "hydro," as having something to do with *water*. Let's begin there.

A simplified explanation of the term HYDROROBICS is easily obtained by dividing the word into its two basic parts. The first part is "hydro," the Greek prefix meaning water. The second part, the suffix "robics," stems from the word aerobics, meaning with oxygen. Therefore, HYDROROBICS is simply exercising in the water aerobically.

"Aerobics" was brought into vogue in the late 1960's by Dr. Kenneth Cooper, who is now recognized as the "father of modern physical fitness." Dr. Cooper conducted extensive research during his tour of duty in the U.S. Air Force on the physiological effect of aerobic exercises on the human body. His research paved the way for writing several books on aerobic exercise, which helped Americans understand the importance of improving the efficiency of our heart and lungs through select endurance-type exercises. Furthermore, he helped Americans answer the question, "How much exercise should I do?" This he did by establishing a fitness evaluation test and an exercise point system which insured that an individual would obtain the necessary aerobic benefits from his exercise program.

In order to understand the aerobic concept you must learn the relationship of the working muscles and their dependency on the heart and lungs to provide oxygen which is needed to help produce energy. Energy is what allows muscles to perform work. This energy is produced by a very complicated process in the cellular tissue of the muscle where oxygen is used to burn available supplies of digested food stuffs. The amount of work that can be performed depends on the availability of oxygen and the supply of food elements in the muscle. Since oxygen is delivered to the muscle via the lungs and the circulatory system, the efficiency of this aerobic transport system will dictate how much work can be performed in the working muscle. How well you can process oxygen is known as the *aerobic capacity*. If you have a poor aerobic capacity, you are only capable of performing at low levels of work, because you cannot process the needed oxygen required for higher levels of work. This phenomenon can be likened to an automobile that performs inefficiently because the malfunctioning carburetor cannot deliver the oxygen necessary to burn gasoline for power in the engine cylinders.

Of all the components of physical fitness, the cardiorespiratory component should be considered the building block of all exercise programs. It is for this reason that many exercise physiologists and physical fitness teachers consider an individual's aerobic capacity to be the *best indicator of physical fitness*. After all, without an efficient heart (or if the heart dies), all other components of physical fitness become unimportant.

While a HYDROROBICS exercise program has a major emphasis on aerobic type exercises, it also includes exercises which develop flexibility, muscular strength and endurance. HYDROROBICS is truly a versatile form of exercise and is viewed by many as an ideal total physical fitness program. Unlike many traditional exercise programs which require the person exercising to develop the components of physical fitness individually and in different facilities (e.g., strength in a weight training room; cardiorespiratory on a track, bicycle, etc.), HYDROROBICS develops all of the fitness components in a single facility. As a matter of fact, several of the components are developed in a single exercise.

After reading the chapter on designing your own HYDROROBICS exercise program, you'll learn that there is a select group of exercises which will help you to improve your aerobic capacity. These exercises have been grouped in such a way as to provide the required intensity for your particular fitness level and will last in total somewhere between several minutes to approximately thirty minutes. The duration and speed at which you perform the exercise combine to produce a truly unique aerobic challenge.

You'll be surprised how high you can get your pulse rate during one of these workouts. Several of our students have experienced pulse counts in the 160-180 beats per minute pulse range, which is more than sufficient (and in some cases too high, depending on your fitness level) to reach the training stimulus (explained in Chapter 1 and other chapters).

A recent study that measured the effects of water exercise showed that 70-77% of maximal heart rate (training pulse rate) could be achieved through moderate workouts of such exercise. This study, published in the March 1983 issue of *Physician and Sports Medicine*, was conducted at the University of Georgia and dealt with measurement of average heart rates, average oxygen uptakes, and average energy expenditures (caloric expenditure!). Results of the study indicated that regular and sufficient exercise of this type would probably improve physical work capacity.

Once you have designed your HYDROROBICS program, your efforts will be channeled into performing the HYDROROBICS exercises in a way that will give you the maximum benefit. You'll have to pay specific attention to performing each exercise correctly and with the proper intensity (balance of speed and duration). For example, to gain the optimum benefit for flexibility you'll want to concentrate on a maximum stretch position. When you do a static stretch you'll have to hold the stretch position for at least an 8-second count. Detailed information will be provided on the difference between a static stretch and a ballistic stretch in the introduction to the exercises. The point made here is that you will want to perform the exercises according to instruction, so that you may reach your specific physical fitness objectives.

Any discussion of HYDROROBICS should include the physical characteristics or properties of the water and the effect they have on exercise. This explanation should be a relatively easy task; almost everyone has been in a body of water at one time or another. Certainly you have experienced the ocean, a lake, or your bath tub. (Got you there. Ha!)

Properties of Water

Water Temperature

One of the more obvious characteristics of water, since it is the first one we tend to react to, is water temperature. How many times have you entered a body of water when it had other than an ideal temperature? Talk about the call of the wild! Most people prefer a water temperature between 78-84 degrees which is the temperature most pool managers strive for in their pools.

From a HYDROROBICS standpoint, the 78-84 degree range is comfortable, although, other temperatures are preferred by people who use HYDROROBICS for its therapeutic effect. It is wise to point out here that HYDROROBICS *per se* does not claim to be a form of hydrotherapy, which is a technical, precise science used in hospitals under the supervision of trained physical therapists. Some HYDROROBICS exercises, however, can have a therapeutic effect on the body because of the nature of the exercise and because it is conducted in a body of water. As you'll find out in a later chapter, a carefully selected group of HYDROROBICS exercises can supplement the rehabilitation of some common injuries and provide people who have specialized medical problems with at least some form of exercise.

Also, exposure to warm water increases our muscles' elastic qualities. This helps to increase our range of movement and tends to prevent muscle injury during exercise.

Water Pressure

The next physical characteristic, *water pressure*, plays a smaller but still significant role in a HYDROROBICS exercise program. As soon as you enter the water you can feel the pressure build up, creating a pressing feeling all over your body. Although this pressure may cause a degree of labored breathing, we tend to adjust to it as we get caught up in the excitement of different water activities.

The primary contribution that water pressure makes to exercise is that it helps to stimulate the body's circulation and causes the respiratory system to work harder. Both of these effects help increase the required overload on the body which is so necessary for improving the quality of our muscles. In a way, we could say your exercise program has begun the moment you enter the water— even though you haven't formally begun your exercise routine. This is an excellent example of how high-risk cardiac patients could begin a very low-keyed program of exercise.

Buoyancy

For some, the third characteristic of water, *buoyancy*, is a blessing in disguise. People who are overweight or possess specialized medical problems that make movement on land more difficult find that water's buoyancy effect permits them to engage in an exercise program. Buoyancy helps to support the body in water and allows for greater ease of movement. This is explained by a law in physics called Archimedes' Principle: *a body immersed in a fluid is buoyed up by a force equal to the weight of the fluid displaced by the body.* This is why you float in water.

Buoyancy simply takes the jolt out of exercising. By applying this theory we can see how a regular jogging fanatic who has injured his knee could continue his exercise program in the water without the threat of increasing the knee injury. Of course his program would have to be modified, but at least he would be able to maintain the physical fitness level he had previously achieved.

Resistance

If we were to name the single-most important physical characteristic of water for improving the quality of our muscles, we would nominate the resistance effect of the water. Resistance is easily experienced, for example, by simply moving an extended arm with your palm open through the water. It feels as if you have some form of weight in your hand. And when you speed up the movement the weight seems to get heavier. This resistance effect produces the overload principle so vital to the HYDROROBICS exercise program.

Massage

Anyone who has experienced a good massage from the hands of a trained masseur/masseuse knows the wonderful relaxed feeling once a body massage has been completed. Can you imagine an exercise program that includes continuous massage? Yes, HYDROROBICS does it again! Although massage is not an actual physical characteristic of water, it is a pleasing benefit created from water resistance and water pressure on the parts of the body that you move through the water. In addition to the soothing effect on your muscles, water massage helps increase the body's surface circulation. This, in turn, makes you feel as if your body is coming alive.

Collectively working together, the physical characteristics of water (temperature, water pressure, buoyancy, resistance) help create a form of exercise that can appeal to a wide variety of people, unlike any other single form of exercise. Regardless of your personal exercise history, one water workout performing HYDROROBICS exercises will give you some idea of why these claims are made about HYDROROBICS. If you have any doubts, read the next section and find out more about the specific benefits of HYDROROBICS.

HYDROROBICS is a popular form of exercise with all types of people.

Benefits of HYDROROBICS

HYDROROBICS has become a popular form of exercise with all types of people. Some of them are people who have always exercised, who enjoy and are active in various sports activities, and who have a lifetime interest in keeping physically fit.

But a lot of people who have adopted HYDROROBICS as their exercise activity do not claim to enjoy exercise or sports. They have just begun to realize that physical fitness should become a part of their lives. There is obviously something very special and exciting about water exercises—even for this kind of person—that makes it so popular.

Are you a part of this last group? Let's look at some of the reasons why you may just be beginning to think about exercise. Let's look at some of the excuses you have made to yourself in the past. Let's also look at some of the benefits of HYDROROBICS that can change those excuses into reasons for becoming a HYDROROBICS enthusiast.

We know you'll want the benefits for yourself. You will want to abandon those excuses! We think we've heard them all.

Benefit #1

We must begin with everyone's favorite excuse for almost anything they don't want to do—"I just don't have the time."

Have you watched a boring television program this week? Have you stopped somewhere after work for an unproductive (and fattening) happy hour lately? Have you wasted 30 minutes or more on a small talk phone conversation in the last few days? more than once? Have you spent time on between-meal snacks? Start adding up the unnecessary time and you'll quickly see that *you do* have time for HYDROROBICS.

All you need for a regular "hydro" program is 40-60 minutes three times a week. Many people use some of their lunch hours for "hydro" at a pool near their place of business. For others it's after work and weekends. If you have small children at home, consider a twice weekly "Mother's day out" program and use that time for you—with "hydro." If you have older children, encourage them to exercise with you. How about early morning? Refreshed and fit is a great way to begin your regular day.

So much for that excuse.

Benefit #2

Another favorite is the one about exercise being hard work. "I work hard all day at my job and then go home to fix dinner for my family. I don't need more work. I just don't have the energy to do more than I do right now."

Wrong. Wrong. Wrong. You're cheating yourself. You will have *more* energy from exercising. And "hydro" is *not* hard work. It's refreshing and it's fun to do.

Amie Izaguirre, age 27, puts it well: "I always feel refreshed when I get out of the water. I don't feel like I've gone and sweated myself out as I would have with some other exercise."

We sometimes joke and say "hydro" is a way to exercise with "no sweat." What we mean, of course, is that even though vigorous movement in the water will cause you to perspire, you don't realize it. You will be working as hard as you want to work for your fitness level. But you will not end your exercise session in the same sweaty condition as a jogger or runner or person doing other land exercises.

You will still have energy to fix dinner, do more work and have some other form of recreation. You will feel refreshed.

Benefit #3

Now that we have mentioned joggers and other exercisers, let's touch on the standard excuse for not exercising, sore muscles.

Sore muscles—who needs them or wants them? Some exercisers believe they aren't getting any benefits unless they have sore muscles. Pain seems to be proof that they're doing something good for themselves.

If you're not into pain, "hydro" is for you. Some exercises that concentrate on the flexibility component of "hydro" will stretch some muscles that you may not have used lately. You may feel some soreness the next day, but not much. Remember, the water is therapeutic and is massaging those muscles as you stretch them. If any form of exercise can be called painless, water exercise is it.

Benefit #4

While we're on the subject of other sports and exercise, perhaps you have heard of the booming business in orthopedic medicine partially caused by an increasing number of sports and recreational injuries, mostly among the ranks of the so-called "Weekend Athlete." Many of them haven't bothered to learn about the exercise they've chosen or to discover how much warm-up activity or proper equipment (such as appropriate shoes) are needed to avoid injury.

If your next excuse is fear of injury, "hydro" again turns into a benefit. We won't claim there has never been some sort of injury in a swimming pool, but water's cushion effect will certainly eliminate the kinds of injuries many other sports and exercise programs seem to generate.

Lawrence Drew, in his early sixties and trying to keep fit, says, "Jogging bothers my ankles and knees, but HYDROROBICS never does. If you come into it with tight muscles, they will be limber before very long and you'll feel limber." Drew feels better than ever and safe from injury.

If you are classifying drowning with the dangers of sports, you'll be happy to know that the deepest water needed for "hydro" is shoulder-deep. See next excuse. HYDROROBICS is safe.

Benefit #5

The word "water" strikes terror in many hearts for a number of reasons.

You may be a non-swimmer with a genuine concern for your safety in water. You may have a problem head of hair that takes hours to fix or turns green at the mere mention of chlorine. HYDROROBICS is still going to be an excellent way for you to become physically fit.

No swimming skill is required for HYDROROBICS. We say this many times throughout the book, but non-swimmers seem to need special reassurance. Check the various exercise chapters in this book, and you will see that every exercise involves holding on to the side of the pool or standing in water no higher than your shoulders. Your head never goes under water unless you choose to put it there.

This also means your hair does not have to get wet. If your hair is long, you may want to pin it up or wear a cap.

Benefit #6

Many of you have very important reasons for not previously exercising. We're responding now to those of you with medical problems which prevented you from making traditional forms of exercise part of your life.

For you, water exercise may be not just a preference but the *only way* to regularly keep physically fit. Hydrotherapy is used all over the world to treat a number of physical ailments, and your physician will probably encourage you to participate in water exercise.

If you have rheumatism, arthritis, multiple sclerosis, chronic back problems, high blood pressure or cardiac problems, you will find you can adjust "hydro" to your particular condition and your specific fitness level. If you are pregnant, "hydro" is an excellent exercise for you and can be adapted to your needs as your body changes.

If you have a temporary physical condition such as strained muscles, torn ligaments, mending broken bones, or extreme obesity (we assume this is a temporary condition), you will find that movement in the water is an excellent way to make a gradual transition into more vigorous activity on the land. You will probably choose to keep "hydro" as a supplement to your other exercise long after your injury is healed or your body is otherwise back to normal.

So if you really haven't been able to exercise for one of these physical reasons, the benefits of water exercise are perfect for you.

Benefit #7

Some of the most active participants in HYDROROBICS are people who thought that their bodies had passed the age of exercise.

You are never too old to exercise. In fact, the more you exercise, the younger you'll look and feel. If you've been sitting on your age as an excuse, you'll want to meet some of the people in this book who are past middle age and feeling great from water exercise.

Remember, you can do things in the water that you can't do on land. The buoyancy of water will support your body and allow for more fluid movement.

Remember Lawrence Drew? He and his wife, also in her sixties, have established a joint program of HYDROROBICS and walking. June Drew says, "I feel more relaxed and better. It ("hydro") makes you feel like you want to take more exercise. After this and every day that we don't exercise, we go out and take a long walk. That's what it's done for us. Nothing's right if you don't feel good." The Drews not only feel good, they're doing something good for both of them and are doing it together.

Benefit #8

If every sport or exercise program you have considered needs some sort of expensive equipment or membership in a club, we think that the benefits of HYDROROBICS are again obvious.

Of course you will need a bathing suit—and a swimming pool. You may be one of the owners of the more than one and a half million home swimming pools in the U.S. If you're not, read on.

Can you get to a college or university, a YMCA or YWCA, an apartment complex or condominium with a pool, a municipal pool, a hotel or motel pool, or someone else's home pool? Most people have access to a swimming pool. One hundred thousand more are building a home pool each year in this country alone. You won't be able to use lack of equipment as an excuse for not trying water exercise.

While we're talking about swimming pools, let's add the recreational environment of pools as an extra benefit. "Hydro" is fun and getting people to exercise in the water with you can make it even more fun.

Benefits #9, l0, etc., etc.

We don't believe you have enough excuses to match all of the physical and emotional benefits of HYDROROBICS. For example, consider how many different exercise activities you would have to participate in to improve aerobic capacity, cardiorespiratory endurance, muscular strength and flexibility (perhaps a combination of jogging or running, weight training, and calesthenics). All of these are benefits of HYDROROBICS.

You can participate in HYDROROBICS no matter what your fitness level or skill. Diane has never been athletic or interested in sports or exercise. Her husband, Jeff, is a runner, plays tennis and swims laps. They often do "hydro" together—both at their own levels and for their own needs. For Jeff it's a supplement to his other forms of exercise; for Diane, her only exercise occurs three times a week in the pool doing HYDROROBICS.

Decide how you would like to benefit from a program of exercise. HYDROROBICS can eliminate all the excuses and give you all the benefits.

Anyone can participate in HYDROROBICS, no matter what their fitness level or skill.

People Speak About the Benefits of HYDROROBICS

Now that we've dealt with some benefits of HYDROROBICS and eliminated all your excuses for not starting an exercise program, let's get more specific about how "hydro" can meet your expectations.

We can tell you what we think HYDROROBICS should do for you. We can give you all the facts about exercise, and water exercise in particular. But we think that the experiences and comments of people who have taken advantage of a "hydro" program for themselves are the best way to convince you that HYDROROBICS is for you. They have a lot of different reasons for choosing "hydro" as their activity, but all of them have had positive results. And that's exactly what we hope will happen to you.

If you're not an athlete, and probably you are not, it is very unlikely that HYDROROBICS will endow you with amazing physical abilities not there before. It can, however, help you achieve the kind of body that is better prepared for other sports and physical activities. So this limitation is merely a matter of degree. You won't be able to leap tall buildings, but you might be readier to learn a good game of tennis or increase the length of time you can run, jog, hike, etc. Or, you might become a more energetic and flexible sexual partner (more on that later!) The other "can not," the one everyone wants to know about, is weight loss. Again, we're talking about a matter of degree. Any increase in physical activity expends calories. If HYDROROBICS is your only physical activity, you'll be burning a small amount of calories in addition to your usual caloric expenditure. That small increase is not going to melt off very many pounds unless you combine it with a change in eating habits or additional exercise. The change in eating habits that we're talking about can be easier than you think. We're not talking about "dieting" forever. A well-balanced diet (that means all types of food—including some sweets and breads) in   moderate amounts can make a difference. (See Chapter 11.)

Diane sets a good example of what an individual *can* do to control weight through HYDROROBICS:

"When I first decided to begin a hydro program, I was about 10 pounds overweight. I thought that most of that extra weight was in the "pot belly" that had developed as a result of lots of good food and absolutely no exercise. I was wrong about the location but not about the reason.

"My approach to keeping a reasonable weight had included periodic 2-week crash diets, in between long stretches of well-balanced meals in great quantities. The clothes that I looked my best in seemed to be the looser styles (sometimes a size 14, but never smaller than a 12).

"The diet that I chose to compliment my "hydro" program was still well-balanced, but the amount was greatly reduced. Coupled with three "hydro" workouts per week for three months, my efforts brought me to my ideal weight and a size 10 dress. A maintenance of that ideal weight involves that well-balanced, reasonable food intake (including desserts and the gourmet foods I enjoy cooking) and the continuation of regular "hydro" workouts.

"Much to my surprise I have continued to lose inches in places (such as arms!) that I didn't know had fat or flab, and the dress size is now down to an 8/9—without additional dieting! I have successfully maintained this new and healthier body for over four years."

You'll note that Diane did not credit HYDROROBICS with her weight loss. She did that herself by first dieting sensibly and changing her basic eating habits—smaller quantities of the food she enjoys. What the "hydro" has done is firm up her body during the weight loss and continue to tone the muscles that had suffered from years of neglect.

"More Examples"

Such minor details as dress sizes can be affected by a regular program of exercise, even without any weight loss. Take Barbara Gaston, age 37, who says. *"I didn't lose much weight, though I was dieting. But I toned up, dropped a size and had to take up the buttons on the shoulder of my bathing suit twice. I finally threw the bathing suit away because it got so big."* Barbara has continued with her "hydro" program of exercise and, we're happy to say, has continued to see results.

Visible results is one of the most exciting things about HYDROROBICS. Seeing positive changes in your body—the way you look and the way you feel—and hearing words of praise and encouragement from others is exciting. Those visible results are what inspire most people to continue with their HYDROROBICS program.

This continuation of an exercise program is the key to any successful approach to fitness. *"I would never stick to an exercise program on land the way I've stuck to this one,"* says Barbara. *"You're tired but you're a relaxed kind of tired and not where you're feeling like you're going to drop dead."*

Seb Cavallero of Riverdale, Georgia was 50 when he began HYDROROBICS. He comments, *"I don't think I'll taper off as fast as I did with other (exercise) programs. I think it's something that I could stay with for a longer period of time."*

For Elizabeth Siceloff of Atlanta, a 58-year-old woman with severe back problems: *"I'm going to incorporate the exercises into my swimming program, so I feel that it's something that can become a part of my life."*

These enthusiastic performers of HYDROROBICS all saw results of one kind or another and wanted to keep on seeing those results. Some of them were trying to lose weight, others to firm up, and most to achieve and maintain a level of cardiorespiratory fitness. Quite a few hoped to exercise in spite of some sort of medical problem that caused traditional forms of exercise to be painful or impossible. (See Chapter 13.)

One young man of 27, Roger Martin of a small town in upstate New York, had always battled a weight problem. By doing regular "hydro" workouts (and reducing his total food intake), he found he could *"eat anything I want to anytime I want to—and I'm getting a suntan at the same time."*

We don't guarantee the suntan, but regular workouts should produce some specific results. So what are some of the specifics we keep mentioning?

Well, what would you like them to be? That's another one of the exciting things about HYDROROBICS. As Susan Deaver, age 35, of Atlanta points out, *"I like being able to individualize my exercise, and HYDROROBICS is the most successful exercise program I've ever been in."*

"Hydro" can work on every part of the body from the neck to the toes. Do you want to reduce your waist measurement? You can do it with "hydro." Would you like to firm up your stomach muscles? You can do it with "hydro." Would you be happier knowing that the loose flesh in your upper arms doesn't have to be there? (This especially happens to women, even those with thin arms.) You can do it with "hydro." Do you think your legs need muscle toning for running or tennis or appearance? By now you know the line. *You* have to do it, but it can be done *with* "hydro."

Of course we don't want to neglect those of you who really don't have a specific problem area to work on. *Pay attention everyone*, because this is the way all of you should and could be using HYDROROBICS.

A body that is in good physical condition, is relatively well-proportioned with a minimal amount of fat, and is generally healthy needs to be kept that way. Just as you can use "hydro" to deal with the "parts" that need improvement, those parts can be maintained as a whole in a way that no other exercise program can offer.

A combination of HYDROROBICS exercises can affect every muscle of the body from the neck to the toes. And almost anyone at any age can do them safely. A specific chapter of this book will touch on medical conditions that might require extra care when participating in an exercise program, but two people you might find interesting come to mind as examples of "anyone can do 'hydro'."

Two Special People

Diane Day, age 27, was expecting her first baby and still taking part in a HYDROROBICS class, with her doctor's approval, in her 7th and 8th months of pregnancy. When a fellow exerciser asked how she was doing, she answered with a big smile and, *"The baby is enjoying this. I can tell."* Certainly the mother was enjoying "hydro" with no ill effects to her body or her child's. Emotionally it seemed to be good for both of them. The baby was a healthy girl.

Jean Johnson is a special person that makes *us* smile! Her story could be used to illustrate several types of people who can success-fully do "hydro" when other exercise seems difficult or impossible.

Jean is not a young woman, and any one of her medical problems would be discouraging to most of us. She's had a bout with cancer, a partial shoulder replacement, and a synovictomy—a removal of fluid that surrounds the joint—on her knee. She has known a great deal of pain and consumed a great deal of medication. But she used her knee surgery and rheumatoid arthritis as excuses to begin a program of HYDROROBICS. After three months of regular "hydro" workouts, there was no hiding the improvement in her physical condition and emotional disposition.

"I feel very much more alive," is quite a statement from someone who could hardly move her body after surgery. *"I have much more flexibility, ease in going up the stairs has increased, and my knees and arms are much more flexible."*

You would find it especially exciting to see Jean Johnson when she boasts that, *"I have improved in every area! It's so wonderful."* The first grade students she teaches would probably agree.

The common thread that runs through the statements of most of the people who have given HYDROROBICS a place in their lives is that they *enjoy it*!! Does this sound like exercise to you?!

Do these people enjoy pain? No, of course not. There isn't any pain from HYDROROBICS. In fact, people who already have pain usually feel better from the therapeutic effect of the water.

What HYDROROBICS addicts do enjoy is improved health and general well-being, improved physical appearance, greater flexibility and resulting ability to attempt new activities (including a few old activities that needed improved bodies), and a sense of pride and accomplishment that only comes from achieving all of the above.

When you "get hooked on 'hydro'," you'll discover that it's easy, it works and it's fun.

Susan Deaver says it best: *"I love the water. I can have a lot of fun and still work hard. It's the most successful exercise program I've ever been in."*

References

Cooper, Kenneth. *Aerobics*. New York: Bantam Books, 1968.

Vickery, Susan R.; Cureton, Kirk J.; and Langstaff, Jamie L. "Heart Rate and Energy Expenditure During Aqua Dynamics." *The Physician and Sportsmedicine*, March 1983, pp. 11-3.

3

QUESTIONS YOU MAY HAVE ABOUT "HYDRO"

WHO CAN DO HYDROROBICS?

Females, males, young people, older people, swimmers, nonswimmers, healthy people, not-so-healthy people, pregnant women, expectant fathers, children tall enough to stand in the water, thin people, not-so-thin people, just about everyone, come to think of it!

If we've left you out, please write to us. You can probably do "hydro" too.

MUST I BE ABLE TO SWIM?

No. All of the regular HYDROROBICS exercises can be done in shallow water and don't require any swimming ability.

Swimmers, however, can enhance their HYDROROBICS program in two ways. Several of the exercises can be modified in deep water for variety or when shallow water is not readily available. Additionally, swimming of laps, with or without flotation devices (i.e., inner tube, kick board), is an excellent method of building endurance and augmenting your fitness plan.

And if you're not a swimmer, you may find that the time you spend in the water enjoying your "hydro" workout will inspire you to learn to swim. After all, several of the exercises (flutter kick, etc.) give you a head start on mastering the skills you need to become a swimmer. Your hydrorobically fit body will be prepared for a variety of new physical activities. Why not swimming?

WHAT IF I'M AFRAID OF THE WATER?

Are you afraid of taking a bath? The deepest water you will ever have to stand in to do "hydro" will be shoulder depth. You will never have to put your head under water. Your face may get splashed, but you won't drown. You might even become comfortable enough with the water to try to learn how to swim. But if you don't, it's okay.

I DON'T HAVE TIME TO GET MY HAIR WET AND FIX IT AGAIN EACH TIME I EXERCISE. CAN I STILL DO "HYDRO"?

Yes. See the answer to the above question. The only part of the body you don't exercise in a HYDROROBICS workout is your head.

WHERE CAN I DO HYDROROBICS?

All "hydro" exercises can be done in a swimming pool. You will need a flat-surfaced pool floor to stabilize your feet and something to hold on to to stabilize your upper body (a gutter rail or pool ladder will do).

Some "hydro" exercises can be done in deeper water (a diving pool where you can hold on to the side or ladder, or the side of an anchored boat with a ladder for gripping).

Some of the aerobic exercises that don't require something to hold on to can be performed on a fairly smooth lake or ocean bottom. But, we don't recommend trying this in wavy water.

Pools are the best place for "hydro," so consider a local "Y," a college or university, a public swimming pool, a neighbor's residential pool, a hotel or motel that might allow the use of their pool, and apartment complexes with swimming pools.

Better yet, build your own pool.

HOW MUCH TIME DOES "HYDRO" TAKE?

To make any exercise program effective, you should find time to do it three times a week for about an hour each session. "Hydro" is no exception to this rule. One 3-hour session won't do it. Three times at 30-45 minutes will be good if you can't spare the full hour.

Many people doing HYDROROBICS take a longer lunch hour twice a week for two of their workouts and fit in the third on the weekend or an evening.

Talk to your employer about the lunchtime option. Many businesses   are encouraging their workers to stay fit and healthy. If you are physically fit, you are likely to have fewer sick days, fewer health insurance claims, and more productive work hours. If enough of us exercise, we will all pay less for our insurance premiums, too.

You and your employer, if you have one, may be interested in the comments of B.J. Clark, a 54-year-old woman from Decatur, Georgia. "Within a month of starting HYDROROBICS I could tell that my endurance and stamina were increasing. I can get through my normal work day now without that midafternoon slump."

Instead of asking how much time "hydro" takes, figure out how much time it will save for you.

I HAVE A MEDICAL PROBLEM THAT HAS KEPT ME FROM EXERCISING. CAN I POSSIBLY CONSIDER "HYDRO"?

Yes. Of course you will get your doctor's permission to exercise (people without a medical problem should do this too—especially after age 35). In other sections of this book you can read about people who have had arthritis, rheumatism, multiple sclerosis, chronic back problems, extreme obesity—the list goes on—and who have been able to exercise successfully with HYDROROBICS.

Water provides a cushion that allows your body to do all sorts of movements that it can not do on land. This is true for healthy people and it is just as true for people with a medical problem.

You will feel better!

I AM PREGNANT. IS IT SAFE TO EXERCISE IN A POOL AND HOW LATE INTO MY PREGNANCY CAN I EXERCISE?

Your doctor will probably tell you it is safe and good for you and your baby to exercise in water during your pregnancy.

There are some "hydro" movements that you won't be able to do because of the shape of your body as it grows. But you'll discover for yourself which exercises are a problem for you.

Most physicians recommend a form of exercise up until labor begins. You should be safe from uterine infection in a swimming pool until the amniotic sac of fluid ruptures, but you'll want to consult with your own obstetrician for recommendations.

HOW WILL I FEEL AFTER A HYDROROBICS WORKOUT?

If you haven't been doing any type of regular exercise activity, you'll probably be tired—the first time! Even if you've been running or doing some other activity limited to specific areas of the body, you'll probably still feel tired. Remember, in a good HYDROROBICS program, you're using muscles in every part of your body; some you may have never exercised before. But with each regular exercise session, you should feel less tired and more exhilarated.

What you should not feel is the sore muscles associated with strenuous exercise. Why? Because HYDROROBICS includes a pre-exercise warm-up session that heats up the muscles and makes them more pliable, preventing muscle strain. Also consider the massaging effect of the water which soothes your muscles from the strain of work. When you're doing HYDROROBICS you don't perform the jerking movements that can cause muscle pulls and are often a part of other forms of exercise.

Even as you increase the length of your workout and the pace of the exercises you choose, that tired feeling will lessen. Why? Because your body will be in better condition, your muscles will have more flexibility, and your endurance factor will have increased.

Most people discover that, if they have been performing regular (2-3 times a week) HYDROROBICS workouts over a period of months, they can physically notice a negative difference in the way they feel when they miss a workout. Certainly part of that feeling is the absence of that psychological "lift" that comes from doing good things for the body. But the person who exercises regularly generates physical energy and eases the tensions of normal living. People who exercise regularly are dealing with stress problems in a positive way. More on that in another section.

As HYDROROBICS workouts become a regular part of your life, you will notice additional changes in the way you feel. The tired feeling will change to one of relaxation and renewal of energy. As other positive benefits (body contouring, weight loss, body flexibility) become evident, the emotional plusses of "hydro" will multiply. It makes sense, if you look at the facts. "Hydro" is easy to do. You don't have sore muscles. You're beginning to feel good physically and emotionally because you're doing good things for yourself. You're starting to look better! Your friends and family are making positive comments about your appearance. Each positive word of encouragement, each glance in the mirror at a newly emerging shape, all add up to more good feelings about you.

If HYDROROBICS is the reason for all this good stuff, you will probably stop feeling just "good" about it and start feeling great!

I HAVE A RECENT INJURY FROM MY FAVORITE SPORT AND I MISS EXERCISE. IS "HYDRO" SAFE FOR ME?

Check with your doctor (about any specific exercise limitations), but you'll probably get an okay to begin water exercise.

For example, once you've had a cast or splint removed from a broken bone, your doctor will encourage you to begin a *mild* form of exercise. As we've said in other sections of this book, there are many things that your body can do in the water that it can't do on land. Water exercise is an excellent way to gradually regain your old fitness level—or better—without risking reinjury.

In addition to exercising recently broken bones, the therapeutic effects of "hydro" can also help such problems as strained muscles, sprained ligaments, tendonitis and other orthopedic problems. (See Chapter 14.)

I'M DIETING. WILL I HAVE THE ENERGY TO EXERCISE?

Yes. For one thing, as you diet you will have less weight to carry and your heart will have to work less and less to pump blood through your body. As you gradually become stronger and your lungs and circulatory system have greater capacity for transporting oxygen, your body will become a more efficient   working unit. You will have more energy than ever before. If you need to lose weight, don't put off dieting because you are exercising. Put off pounds—and inches—instead. Your physician will advise you on how much and how quickly.

As a matter of fact, medical researchers have found that exercising while dieting is preferred. People who diet without exercise tend to not only lose fat, but also lose muscle! This is not healthy. If you have lost muscle and then regain weight, you will be gaining fat. Yuk!

The best part about exercising and dieting simultaneously is that the muscle toning benefits of "hydro" will minimize the flabby skin that can result from dieting. Remember, muscle weighs more than fat. So don't be discouraged if the numbers on the scale and the loss of inches on your body don't seem to correlate right away. As you lose fat and build muscle, it is possible to become firmer and trimmer without actually losing much weight. How much weight you lose will depend on how much you needed to lose and how carefully you are monitoring your food intake. (See Chapter 11.)

Even if you don't lose by the scale, you will look and feel better as you begin the muscle toning process. Long after she stopped   losing weight, people would ask Diane if she had lost more weight. She was still losing inches. They weren't looking at the scale with her, but they could see how much better she looked. She doesn't diet anymore, but she has plenty of energy for exercising. You will too.

YOU'RE KIDDING WHEN YOU SAY THAT "HYDRO" CAN IMPROVE MY SEX LIFE, RIGHT?

Wrong!

There are some "hydro" exercises that will definitely improve flexibility and strength in the areas of your body that are most used during sexual activity. (See Chapter 17.)

But in general, a healthier, more physically fit and more attractive you will also be a sexier you.

Pot bellies are not sexy. Flabby flesh is not sexy. Shortness of breath is not sexy. Lack of energy is not sexy. As Diane's husband tells us, "She's trimmer, she has more energy. She feels better about herself."

That's sexy.

WHAT WOULD "HYDRO" DO FOR ME THAT I DON'T ALREADY GET FROM SWIMMING LAPS FOR EXERCISE?

A HYDROROBICS program works all the muscles from the neck to the toes in several different ways.

Swimming laps is an excellent way to build up endurance and strength in the arms and legs and cardiorespiratory system. It's a good supplement to your HYDROROBICS exercise plan.

"Hydro" also builds endurance and strength—but in more than the arms and legs. What have you done for your *toes* lately? It also improves flexibility, tones the muscles—especially in that notorious mid section—and improves the cardiorespiratory system.

Have you ever gotten bored swimming laps? You're more likely to stick with "hydro," because it's fun and never boring.

WHAT IF I FEEL SILLY DOING SOME OF THE AEROBIC EXERCISES AT A PUBLIC POOL?

Some people have found that they got over feeling silly quickly when people asked them what they were doing and then asked to be shown the exercises.

Most people who are at a swimming pool are either there to swim or to splash around and have fun. The swimmers will usually see "hydro" as a great way to warm up before serious swimming or in place of one of their swimming sessions.

The other group will respond to the fact that "hydro" is fun.

Don't worry about the very few who don't fall into either category.

Your other option, of course, is to get a friend to join you in your "hydro" adventure. Two people doing "hydro" never feel silly.

To people who are considering a HYDROROBICS program, the initial cost can either be virtually nothing or several thousand dollars.

SPECIAL CONSIDERATIONS

It's fairly safe to say that one of the first questions most people ask when considering a new activity or sport is, "What equipment do I need and how much will it cost?" Many activities can cost the consumer up to several hundred dollars or more, while others may only represent a modest outlay of under $50.00, e.g. a pair of running shoes for the jogger or roadrunner.

To people who are considering a HYDROROBICS program, the initial cost can either be virtually nothing or several thousand dollars.

Availability of Pools

If you are just wanting to start a HYDROROBICS program, you will obviously need access to a pool. Let's begin with the most expensive approach—building your own private home swimming pool. This can range in cost from about $1,000 for an above ground pool to $5,000 or more for an in-ground pool.

Those of you who already have a private home pool only need to read this book and get started. What about the person who doesn't go the private-home-pool route?

Well, considering there are over 1,729,000 private home pools, 51,354 municipal pools, and over 295,700 pools in YMCA's, YWCA's, health and fitness centers, motels, apartment complexes and universities, you should have access to a pool in your neighborhood. If you are struggling to find one, perhaps you can persuade your neighbors to start a "hydro" program with you in *their* pool. You'll be surprised how many people will try something new if you're willing to help them along.

Types of Pools

Although you may not have the luxury of selecting the type of pool in which to do your "hydro" workout, you should be aware of the many different pool types and design features that may affect your exercise program.

Pools come in many different sizes and shapes, but the most important features to be concerned with are water depth and the gripping surface for stabilizing in the water. Since most pools have a graduated water depth, e.g., 3-12 feet, you won't have any difficulty in adjusting to the required water level for each exercise. Diving wells in institutional settings have an average depth of approximately 12 feet. This is not desirable for "hydro" although several exercises don't require a standing position.

Many HYDROROBICS exercises require you to stabilize the upper part of your body, so you will need to "grip" some part of the pool. Some pools have a gutter or skim trough near the top of the pool wall which you can grip. Otherwise you can use either the top edge of the pool, where the wall meets the deck, or the ladder.

Stabilizing or gripping will cause your muscles to tire at first, but as you develop these muscles (isometric contractions) you will be able to "hang on" longer.

Water Temperature

Every time we enter a pool we're concerned about the water's temperature. In the summer we prefer cool temperatures, in the winter warmer temperatures.

Most pool managers try to maintain a standard temperature between 78 degrees and 81 degrees in outdoor pools and between 82 degrees and 84 degrees in indoor pools. Unlike home pool owners, the public does not have the privilege of regulating these temperatures to their liking. The homeowner has the advantage, particularly if there is a medical condition that requires a specific water temperature, e.g., arthritis.

Medical Checkup

When you start an exercise program, the American Medical Association recommends that you obtain medical clearance from your physician. This is especially important if you are over 35 years of age and have not vigorously exercised for years. This standard was developed because too many Americans have died from undetected medical problems during exercise. We know many people who don't like to go to their doctors for this sort of thing. Remember, your life may be at stake—so *at least* phone your physician and discuss your exercise interests.

If you have a diagnosed medical condition, it is even more important to consult your physician or specialist. You will probably be able to exercise but with some type of limitation. If you have a *serious* medical problem, e.g., cardiac, you need to start your exercise program in a facility that offers special medical supervision, e.g., a cardiac rehabilitation center.

But, if you receive a clean "bill of health," you can begin your exercise program now.

Use of Water Aids

Once you establish your HYDROROBICS program and progress to a fairly high level of physical fitness, you may be interested in using water aids. Water aids such as hand paddles will help you increase the overload effect as you exercise. Swimming fins are excellent to use in the *Wide Leg Kick*. We have used "divers weight belts" in our class with good results. This works particularly well in the aerobic exercises. Weight belts have also helped exercisers who are extremely bouyant in the water. They help these people stabilize during exercise.

Water aids can be purchased at your local pool distributor or athletic sporting goods store.

Music

Music can add spice to your life and life to your exercise! Exercising to music adds variety to a routine repeated each workout. You might enjoy just playing a radio at poolside. Or be more sophisticated— select music which has a specific rhythm to match the tempo of an exercise. Some of our friends have recorded their whole aerobic workout to music. It's more enjoyable, they say, and what's more, it helps them to keep the necessary intensity of the exercise.

Water Games

If you are part of a class or have a group of friends with whom you exercise, it is a nice change of pace to play water games. You might like to occasionally substitute your regular aerobic workout with water games. Perhaps as your fitness level improves, you could cap off a "hydro" workout with a game or two—for extra fitness! Believe us, games like water polo afford great aerobic benefits.

Consider the following:

- Kickboard Races
  Using a kickboard or some other flotation device, race back and forth in a pool according to a pre-determined distance or number of lengths.
- Inner Tube Races
  Inner tubes have always been fun in the water. You can devise races with inner tubes with a variety of body positions on the tube, e.g., hanging through the "donut" hole, flat on the tube either face up or face down, or a sitting position. The inner tube has a drag factor which requires more energy from you as you either kick with your legs or use your hands in paddle-like movements.
- Other Games
  Several aquatic textbooks on the market include a chapter on water games and can give you many new ideas. It might also be fun to create your own games. You're only limited by your imagination.

Breast Support

Many large-breasted women in our classes have had problems staying in their bathing suits during the more active aerobic exer-

When you start an exercise program, the American Medical Association recommends that you obtain medical clearance from your physician.

cises. As entertaining as this may be for the spectators at the pool, we do not recommend promoting "hydro" in this way.

Even small breasts need proper support during vigorous exercise activity. For this reason, we suggest a one-piece bathing suit that crosses and supports the breasts. Several popular leotard manufacturers now market this type of garment for easy movement in the water. A wide color selection is available, and you will be comfortable, attractive and secure as you exercise.

5

DESIGNING YOUR PERSONALIZED PROGRAM

We would like to congratulate you. Not because you've managed to get this far in our book, but because you have decided to exercise and are taking the initial steps toward starting a HYDROROBICS program. Your first step will be to determine how fit you are at present. You need to know your strengths and weaknesses in the various components of physical fitness so that you can provide for the development of the weak areas in your total exercise program. Don't forget, you'll also want to consider some specific personal fitness goals—e.g. body contouring for a more shapely figure, improving sports performance or supplementing the rehabilitation of an injury—and to incorporate them into the design of your overall program.

Physical Fitness Tests

The tests to be used will help you measure the various components of physical fitness. Please keep in mind that your test results are just a rough estimate of your physical fitness. The tests have certain limitations because several human factors can influence the results, e.g., how well you're motivated on a given test day, your psychological and biological makeup, your daily biorhythms, recent injuries, health problems, etc. It is important to try your best on each test so that you will obtain fairly accurate results.

Physical fitness tests and instructions on how to administer them appear later in this chapter.

HYDROROBICS Fitness Levels

Once you have completed the physical fitness tests, you will be able to determine your exercise fitness level using the results. This will help you exercise at your appropriate ability level. There's nothing worse than participating in an exercise program which is too strenuous. If it is too taxing, you will probably push the "panic button" after two or three workouts and stop exercising for good.

Each exercise lists the three fitness levels and the suggested number of repetitions you should perform to gain a benefit from that exercise. When an exercise requires too large a number of repetitions, we have instead used a specific time interval to guide you in the proper intensity of the exercise.

Three fitness levels or categories of fitness have been identified for your use and are explained as follows:

Fitness Level A

You would be placed in this level if you had scored above average on your fitness tests. It indicates that you have already achieved a high fitness level from previous exercise programs or by participating in high energy sports. You are probably interested in exercise in order to maintain your current level of fitness or to improve a particular fitness component needed in a specialized sport skill.

Fitness Level B

This level is for someone moderately active who has scored average on most of the fitness tests. While you value the benefits of exercise, your approach to exercising regularly is inconsistent due to your work schedule or other personal reasons.

Fitness Level C

Fitness Level C is intended for those of you who haven't exercised for at least one year, lead a sedentary lifestyle, or have some form of health risk factor, e.g., high blood pressure, emphysema, high levels of stress, etc. In any event, you need to begin exercise at a low pace and pay particular attention to medical and physical warning signs.

In addition to finding your exercise fitness level, the fitness tests can be readministered periodically to determine your progress. Good results on your fitness tests may serve to be a motivational factor. If you retest yourself at intervals and find that you are not meeting your desired goals, then you should take a close look at your methods of exercise. Poor progress may be a result of not performing your exercise routinely or not meeting the required intensity in each exercise. Remember, "You will get out of exercise what you put into it."

Pre-Test Information

Before you self-administer the individual tests, let's consider some important general information and guidelines that will help you prepare for the physical fitness evaluation.

Doctor's Approval

We think it's fair to say that most people would not rush to a physician for an approval on each decision they make in life. However, if you're going to exercise, it is wise to discuss the nature and type of exercise program you intend to participate in with your physician. If you have a known health problem, your physician should be able to help you modify your HYDROROBICS program as needed.

The American Medical Association strongly recommends that any individual over the age of 35 years should have a complete physical examination before starting an exercise program. The examination normally includes an exercise stress test which is monitored by an electrocardiogram under the supervision of a cardiologist. In this way, most "hidden" heart problems can be detected and provided for in a detailed exercise prescription by the cardiologist. We know that you will at least "check in" with your doctor.

"Psyching Up" for Your Fitness Test

Besides needing some very basic equipment and comfortable clothing, you will need to be psychologically prepared for the tests.

Chances are you will be a little doubtful and even a bit nervous at the prospect   of finding out what kind of shape you're really in. Can't handle bad news, eh? Well, maybe you'll surprise yourself and not be as bad off as you think.

John, a perpetual procrastinator about exercise, tried to start an exercise program on several occasions. Unfortunately, when he got to the fitness tests, he would always "chicken out." Last year we finally convinced him to give it a try. After scoring average on several of the tests, his whole attitude changed. When he realized that he didn't compare so badly to other Americans in his age category, a new self-confidence and determination to exercise emerged.

We use this example because we want you to know that not everyone will score miserably on the fitness tests. True, some of you will, but that's no reason to be overly discouraged.

It's better to take the attitude that you're going to improve on your weak areas and add to the general quality of your life.

You will need the following:

- Watch with second hand.
- 12″ step bench.
- Yard stick.

Clothing selection should be basic and include a pair of tennis shoes, gym-type shorts, and a light shirt. Women have additional dress options; for example, leotards are very popular among women who exercise. Where you live and whether or not you do your testing indoors or outdoors are important considerations; you will need to dress appropriately for the weather conditions.

Designing Your Personalized Program

Okay, let's get started! All you need to do is follow the four procedures listed below and you will have a personalized HYDROROBICS exercise program.

Step #1. Take The Physical Fitness Test

(Use the Fitness Profile Form in the Appendix to record your results.)

Cardiorespiratory Endurance — Step Test

- Obtain a bench or other object (box, stairs, etc.) 12″ high.
- Work with a partner.
- You will need to maintain a step cadence of 96 beats/minute or 24 steps/minute.

- The stepping method should be as follows: "step-up"-one, two; and "step-down"-three, four, for a total of four movements. NOTE: Practice this cadence so that you perform 24 steps/minute or one complete step-up and down in 2.5 seconds.
- When you're ready to start, your partner should give you the signal to begin as he or she starts the watch. Have the partner help you with the rhythmic cadence by counting out loud—1,2,3,4.
- Continue the stepping exercise for 3 minutes. As soon as the 3 minutes are up, sit down and count your pulse for 10 seconds (you should start the count within 5 seconds after the exercise).
- To get your minute pulse multiply the number of beats obtained in the 10 second count by 6.

HELPFUL HINTS:
1. Practice the stepping cadence before you take the actual test. Do a few one-minute practice sessions, but rest at least 10 minutes before taking the test.
2. If you lose the cadence, keep working and try to get back with the rhythm. As long as you don't lose it too often during the test, your results should be valid.
3. Be sure to fully straighten your leg at the knee when stepping up on the bench.
4. Measure your pulse at the carotid artery just below the jawbone and next to the Adam's Apple.
5. Be sure your bench is secure so that you don't fall during the test.

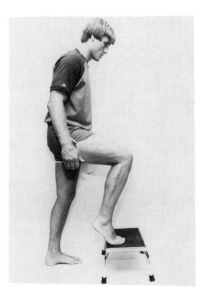

Flexibility Test — Bend and Reach

- Place a box or other object about 8-10″ high and 12″ or more wide securely against a wall.
- Sit upright with double legs extended and your feet flat against the box.
- With both arms extended in front of you (one hand on top of the other) reach *slowly* toward your shoes, as far as possible. Stay in this stretched position for at least 3 seconds.
- Have your partner measure (with a ruler), the distance the tip of your fingers extend either before or beyond the bottom of your feet (or edge of the box your feet are against). If your fingers extend beyond the bottom of your shoes, it will be a positive value (e.g., + 4); if they don't reach your shoes, it will be a negative value (e.g., − 2″). Record these measurements to the nearest half inch.

HELPFUL HINTS:
1. Do some stretching warm-up exercises for your back before taking the test.
2. Do not bounce forward, or you may hurt yourself.
3. Keep your legs *straight* with knees "locked" in place.

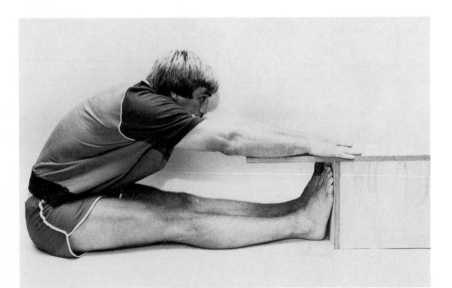

Muscular Strength and Endurance — Bent Knee Sit-Ups

- Lie flat on the floor on your back. Raise your knees so that your upper leg is at a right angle with your lower leg. Keep your feet on the floor.
- Have your partner kneel and hold your feet.
- When your helper tells you to start, perform as many bent knee sit-ups as you can to do a cadence of 60 sit-ups per minute (or 1 sit-up per second). When you break the cadence, record the number of sit-ups done to this point. Practice the cadence in the same manner as you did for the cardiorespiratory step test.
- Your partner should count the number of sit-ups you perform and help you keep the cadence.

HELPFUL HINTS:
1. One full sit-up equals one sit-up-and-lie down movement.
2. You must at least sit-up to a vertical position with your back.

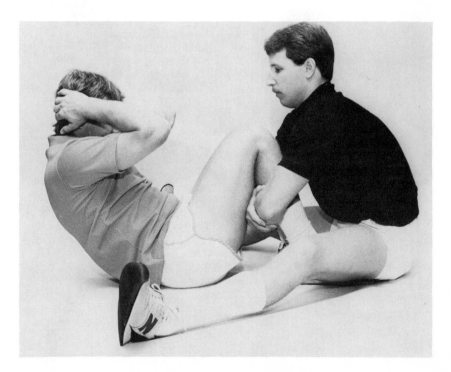

Body Composition — Pinch Test

A popular method of determining the percent of body fat is with the use of skinfold calipers. Since this instrument is not readily available to the public, a more simple but less accurate method is used for this test.

- You will need to pinch a portion of the skin (a skinfold) under one of your arms just beneath the bicep muscle. The site of the skin fold should be midway between the elbow and your armpit.
- While pinching the skin and fat, pull or "tug" the skinfold away from the muscle. Measure (approximate) the thickness of this skinfold as best as you can.

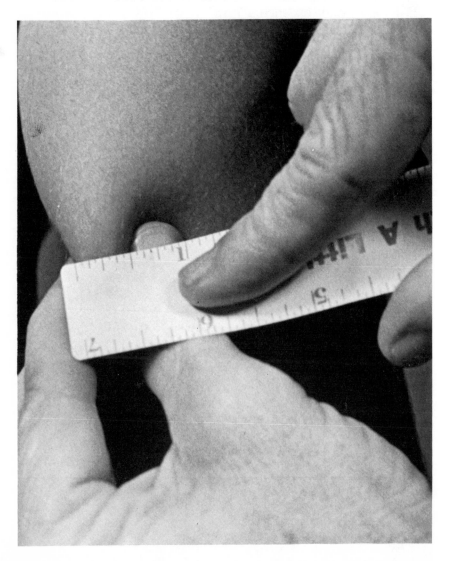

Step #2. Determine Your Physical Fitness Level

Once you have completed all of the tests, you will want to record your results on the Fitness Profile form available in the Appendix. Next, you'll need to combine all of these scores for a total score.

To determine your HYDROROBICS Fitness Level, simply find the range of your total score—and you have your fitness level.

Step #3. Establish Specific Fitness Goals

If you are exercising for a specific reason (be it body contouring, losing weight or some other) as well as developing total physical fitness, you will need additional information to complete your personalized exercise program.

Depending on your specific fitness goal, you will want to select specific lower, mid and upper body exercises, then concentrate your effort on these. For example, if you're interested in firming up your waist and hips to become more shapely, you need to select mid and lower body exercises that work these areas. Each exercise lists the body parts it affects.

For your waist you might select the *Double Leg Lifts*, *Windshield Wiper,* and modified *Scissors Cross.* Instead of performing one set of ten repetitions of each exercise you might perform two or three. More information on this appears in the upcoming section on "The Standard Workout."

For further information on specific fitness goals, consult the chapters in Part III.

In order to develop a personalized program, you should establish specific fitness goals.

Step #4. Calculate Your Training Pulse

Are you familiar with the expression, "All that work for nothing?" It's not a nice thought, but there are many people involved in exercise programs who do not obtain the physical benefits that they want and can get. Have you ever had a friend who has been exercising for several months but hasn't improved aerobic capacity, or slowed down the pulse rate, or lost some unwanted weight, or isn't running any greater distance than in the beginning? We have! And the reason is simple. This person doesn't exercise enough!

Two of the most often asked (and intelligent) questions about exercise are, "How much exercise should I get?", and "How do I know when I should stop exercising?" In order to find the specific answers, you need to know something about what is called the *training stimulus*. The muscles in your body can only grow and become stronger if you overload them when you exercise. How much you overload them is important. Most exercise authorities agree that you must subject the muscles to at least 60% of their maximum capabilities if you are to obtain the training stimulus and improve the quality of your muscles. As a general guideline you should exercise at a rate of 60-85% of your maximum target heart rate in endurance activities. This range is called the Training Pulse Rate Zone. Pulse rate has been proven to increase linearly with the body's energy demands during exercise. That's why pulse rate is used as a simple means to measure physiological stress on the body.

If you are just beginning to exercise, you will appropriately elect to work at the 60% target rate. If you are a conditioned athlete, you will probably be training at the upper limit or 85% target rate. In either case, exercising in the training pulse rate zone will insure that you are performing sufficient aerobic work which will help you improve your cardiorespiratory system.

Thanks to a Finnish exercise researcher, Karvonen, a simple method of determining your training pulse rate has been devised. The method uses the difference between your resting pulse rate and the maximal heart rate as a base value which you multiply by the preferred training percentage level (e.g., 60 or 70 or 85%). The formula and worksheet for calculating your target heart rate appear in Appendix A. Calculate yours now!

An example of calculating the 60% target heart rate for a man who is 30-years-old and has a resting pulse rate of 70 is as follows:

220-30 (age) = 190 Maximum Pulse Rate (MPR)
190 (MPR)-70 (Resting Pulse) = 120 Pulse Rate Reserve (PRR)
120 (PRR) × 60% = 72
72 + 70 (Resting Pulse) = 142 or Training Pulse Rate

Whenever this 30-year-old man exercises in an aerobic activity, he should exercise at an intensity that will increase pulse rate to 142 beats per minute. A popular method of determining your pulse rate during exercise is to momentarily stop exercising, count your carotid artery's palpitations for ten seconds, then multiply this number by six (6) to determine your minute pulse count.

The Standard Workout

The standard HYDROROBICS workout includes exercises to develop all the components of physical fitness. Your fitness level will determine how long your exercise workout will last. The following standard workout is suggested.

Warmup

Proper warmup is necessary to help prepare your muscles for forceful work and prevent injury.
- Perform 1-2 minutes of aerobic exercises to warm up your muscles and prepare them for strenuous exercise. Select two or three of your favorite aerobic exercises such as *Straight Leg Kick*, *Cossack*, etc.
- Select exercises from the body group that will help you to stretch muscles in the major muscle group, e.g., *Hip Dip*, *Universal*, *Figurehead*, etc.

Aerobic Exercise

Perform aerobic exercises to develop cardiorespiratory fitness.
- Select exercises from the aerobic group. You may eventually identify a group of favorites.
- Be sure to allow a few minutes to "cool down" after this session, allowing the body to *gradually* return to normal.

The Body Exercises   (Lower, Mid, Upper)

These exercises will help you develop flexibility, muscular strength and muscular endurance.
- You might try to perform all the suggested exercises in each area or select specific ones in connection with your *specific* fitness goals.

Cool Down

Every exercise workout should have a cool down period to allow the blood, which has been directed to the extremities, to return to the

heart. Otherwise your blood will tend to "pool" in the extremities and cause you possibly to get dizzy and black out.
- Walk around the pool or do very light aerobic exercises for a few minutes. Your pulse rate should recover to approximately 100 beats per minute.

See the section on "Exercise Guidelines" for more information on the standard workout.

Suggested HYDROROBICS Workouts

To help you get started with your personalized HYDROROBICS program, we are suggesting a complete workout for each fitness level. These workouts appear in the Appendix.

Keep in mind that these are only suggested and that you may modify each workout to suit your interests. First, notice that the duration varies for each level. This is because a person who is more fit can handle a greater overload on the muscles.

When to Change Fitness Levels

As your muscles continue to adjust to the overload principle, you become stronger and improve the various components of physical fitness. Not everyone will make the same gains in the same areas or at the same rate, but you should begin to see results within five to six weeks of your program. Often people in our classes tell us that they have lost inches from their waists, or are able to walk   four flights of stairs without huffing and puffing. These are examples of some tangible consequences that you might experience.

The real test of your progress is when you retest yourself on the fitness tests. While some improvement may be realized in one or more fitness components, little may be noticed in others. If this is the case, review the way in which you perform your exercises. Perhaps you are not applying all the guideline suggestions (which will appear in the next section) or maybe you're missing part of your workout more frequently than you should.

The time to upgrade your fitness level is when your retest has accumulated the necessary additional points to place you in the next fitness level. Again, we're all different and some of us might take longer to advance than others. If this is true for you, be patient and continue with your *commitment* to your program. You will eventually receive the big reward—moving up to the next fitness level, C to B or B to A.

How HYDROROBICS Affects Fitness

Remember, you are exercising in water and must take advantage of its physical properties. Before we discuss the specific guidelines, you should be aware of how water works for you in developing the physical fitness components. In this way you can take advantage of the water's physical properties.

Cardiorespiratory (C-R) Endurance

Reading Chapter 1, you learned that cardiorespiratory endurance is developed by overloading large muscle groups for extended periods of time (e.g. 30 minutes). This will result in improvement of your aerobic capacity (the ability of the heart and lungs to process oxygen to the working tissues). The water's resistance is solely responsible for helping you attain the necessary overload. The faster or more forceful the movements you make with your body parts, the greater the overload on your muscles. That's why when you perform your aerobic exercises you should move vigorously, not just glide through the exercise. How fast you'll want to move will depend on your fitness level and the number of repetitions or time required for each exercise.

You should also emphasize keeping the largest surface area of the body part presented to the direction of the movement. If you are swinging your arms as in the *Mae West*, you will keep your palms open to the direction of movement. A large surface area presented to the direction of movement commands more force or overload.

Flexibility

This component is least affected by the water. You have to make this one work. Flexibility is improved by stretching your muscles as far as possible in both static and dynamic stretching. No matter what exercise you're doing for flexibility, you need to concentrate on the proper stabilizing technique. For example, if you're doing the *Windshield Wiper*, it will be extremely important to stabilize your back against the wall as you swing and hold your legs in the stretch position. If you let your back move away from the wall, you will lose part of the stretch factor.

The one benefit of doing flexibility exercises in water is that the water movement over the body produces a massage effect which can induce relaxation and aid in surface circulation. Also, pool water temperatures may help people with specific health problems.

Muscular Strength

Development of muscular strength is accomplished by overloading the skeletal muscles in the same manner you develop your cardiorespiratory endurance. Here again, the water's resistance plays a significant role.

You may develop your maximum muscular strength potential through HYDROROBICS, but you'll have to work very hard. Most people are more interested in muscle tone (a balance of strength and tight, smooth muscles on your frame) than in brute strength. Because of this, it is suggested that you perform eight to ten repetitions of each exercise (where repetitions apply) and do them with progressive resistance or force. This means if you select the *Pendulum* exercise, you should do the first few repetitions with moderate effort and finish the last few with all-out effort. If you want to just build strength, you will perform each repetition with maximum force. As strength increases, you may increase the amount of force used in each repetition, e.g., 60 to 70%.

Muscular Endurance

Muscular endurance is best obtained by subjecting the skeletal muscles to a weight or force with repeated movements. Most muscular endurance programs recommend that you perform ten or more repetitions with at least 50-60% effort. Again, the water's resistance will provide the required overload needed to develop muscular endurance. You should perform each repetition with continuity, not allowing the muscle to relax between repetitions.

The water's massage effect will help soothe the muscles as they go through the endurance workout. Massage will also help limit the amount of muscle soreness endurance work usually causes.

As your muscles adjust to a specific level of effort (force of movement) during your training program, you may increase the percent of effort, e.g, 60 to 70%, to increase the overload. In this way, you can develop the maximum endurance capabilities of your skeletal muscles.

Body Composition

From the practical viewpoint, body composition simply means having the right balance between fat and muscle—without being overweight. If you have too much fat, the only way to lose some of it is to strike a balance between diet and exercise. You need to burn calories—especially calories stored as fat! Participate in cardiorespiratory endurance type activities that demand large amounts of calories for energy. Aerobic exercises will get at those stored fats and help you to create that shapely figure.

Exercise Guidelines

The following is a list of specific guidelines to help you with your HYDROROBICS exercise program.

Start Your Program Slowly

Remember, you don't want to exhaust or hurt yourself. If you're just beginning an exercise program, your muscles may not be conditioned and are thus susceptible to injury. Practice moderation and listen to your "pain response mechanism." If you hurt—stop or limit your exercise!

Don't Cheat!

That's right—don't cheat! It's easy to glide through the "hydro" exercises. You have to make the water work for you! Come on and "put something into it" so you can "get something out of it!" For example, always try to keep your palms open to the direction of movement whenever you use your arms.

Use Progressive Resistance

When you perform exercises as repetitions (e.g., 10 repetitions equal one set), increase the amount of force to each repetition as you progress in the set. The last three repetitions of a set should involve near maximum force. This will help you to develop strength as well as endurance.

Breathing

You should establish a good rhythmic breathing pattern in each exercise. Breathing in itself is an exercise if it is forceful. Since you use only part of your vital capacity (total breathing capabilities) during normal activity, exercise will allow you to use your breathing mechanism to its fullest. This will help you develop your aerobic capacity. Remember, inhale on expanding or relaxing movements and exhale during forceful ones.

Posture

Good posture helps alleviate unwanted stress on your spinal column and other body parts. If you already have poor posture, now is the time to improve it—during "hydro." As you concentrate on posture, your main objective will be to reduce the stress on the lower back. This can be done by avoiding the extreme arch position of the back and by tightening your abdominal muscles and buttocks. The result will be that your pelvis will tilt backwards and your spine will straighten. Try to keep this position during exercises that require you to be in a standing position.

Training Pulse Rate

It's important that you attain your training pulse rate (TPR) during the aerobic exercises. At first it will be a "trial and error" method of learning just how much intensity you'll need in order to reach the TPR. Should your pulse be 15 or 20 beats below the TPR when you take a pulse count, you'll know that you have to add a little more vigor to your exercise. Once you establish a "perceived" intensity, you won't have to count so often.

Also, be sure you adjust your TPR once you have adapted to a particular training level. You'll know when this happens. For example, if you have been training at a pulse rate of 140 beats per minute for 20 minutes of aerobic exercises and in eight weeks your pulse drops to, let's say, 128 beats per minute for the same 20 minutes (same intensity of exercise), it's time to adjust or increase the overload. Either add more time to your aerobic workout or increase the intensity.

Frequency of Workouts

Exercise must become a permanent part of your lifestyle. We all know that there are many facets to our lives, and competition exists between each of them. Priorities dictate our daily schedules, and those that are financially based always seem to win out. Well, it's time for each of us to realize that we come first. Our families, professional colleagues and friends all depend on us. We depend on ourselves. That's why our health is our most prized possession. Exercise helps improve and maintain optimum health.

Exercising three to four times a week helps develop an adequate level of physical fitness. Since we are "creatures of habit," HYDROROBICS should become a standard activity in your weekly routine. Once established, your exercise workout sessions will become as important to you as those three "square meals" you depend on each day.

HYDROROBICS and Eating

Since you will be both exercising and in the water, it would be advisable not to eat for at least an hour or more before you exercise.

Exercise Cautions

Just to be on the safe side, we would like to discuss some specific precautions we think you should take during your "hydro" workout. The following cautions will help you have a safe and pleasant exercise experience.

Low back Problems

If you have a low back problem you should be aware of the following HYDROROBICS exercises:

- Universal
- Figurehead
- Double Leg Lift
- Fire Hydrant
- Quad Stretch
- Pendulum

These exercises will help to strengthen your back, but can also cause potential injury if you use too much force. This is especially true if you have weak abdominal muscles. Go slow at first, and keep good body alignment.

Isometric Exercises

You should know that isometric exercises can be dangerous if you hold your breath for an extended period of time. Commonly called the "Valsalva Maneuver," the glottis in the larynx is forced closed when you don't breathe properly. This causes the thoracic pressure to increase and interfere with arterial blood flow to the brain. It can lead to your "blacking out." That's why it's important to exhale slowly during forceful movements allowing thoracic pressure to be relieved.

Cardiac patients have to take special precautions if they elect to do any isometric type exercises, since studies have shown that isometrics tend to elicit irregular heart beats.

Heat Stroke and Heat Exhaustion

If you elect to exercise in an outdoor pool in the summer, you may need to consider the possibility of heat stroke and heat exhaustion, particularly if you are older. While it may seem highly unlikely that these would occur in the water—they can happen. We advise you to "brush up" on their symptoms in your favorite first aid manual.

References

Corbin, Charles B.; Powell, Linus J.; Lindsey, Ruth; and Tolson, H. *Concepts in Physical Education*. Dubuque, Iowa; William C. Brown Company Publishers, 1981.

Getchell, Bud. *Physical Fitness—A Way of Life*. New York: John Wiley and Sons, 1983.

The Committee on Exercise. *Exercise Testing and Training of Apparently Healthy Individuals: A Handbook for Physicians*. Dallas, Texas: American Heart Association, 1972.

Vitale, Frank. *Individualized Fitness Programs*. New Jersey: Prentice-Hall, Inc., 1973.

Wilmore, Jack H. *Athletic Training and Physical Fitness: Physiological Principles and Practices of the Conditioning Process*. Boston: Allyn and Bacon, Inc., 1977.

PART TWO

THE HYDROROBICS EXERCISES

THE HYDROROBICS EXERCISES

This is it! This is what the book is all about—the HYDROROBICS exercises!

Remember the saying, "You get out of it what you put into it!" Before you get into the water, we want to be sure you are really ready to get the most benefit out of your HYDROROBICS program. That means you are going to have to put something into your program, too.

It is easy to cheat at HYDROROBICS. No one can really tell what you are doing under the water. Only you will know if you are gliding through the water or forcefully moving the parts of your body. You can perform the exact same motions either way-with or without force. You won't be as tired if you try the easy way to do "hydro." You also won't see many results.

So, before you get in the water, decide what you want to accomplish. If you'd like to play and splash, have a good time. If you'd also like to improve your physical fitness and appearance, work. We think you'll also have a good time doing it.

Huff and Puff

Proper breathing as you exercise is a must! You will be most aware of your breathing patterns as you do the more vigorous aerobic exercises. But breathing deeply and rhythmically is an important part of every exercise.

Establish a breathing pattern for yourself with each exercise. Consistently inhale each time you perform a certain motion, consistently exhale each time you perform a different part of the motion. If you're doing an up and down motion, inhale on the up and exhale on the down. It's simple.

Learn to establish breathing patterns when you first do the aerobic exercises, or any exercise that includes a forceful motion alternating with a less forceful one. Exhale on the forceful motion (exhaling helps you put more *push* into the force), and inhale on the recovery aspect of the motion.

Breathing patterns and the intensity of the exercise have an effect on the training pulse rate you achieve for each workout. Of course, what you're trying to do is improve your cardiorespiratory system. If you're not sure what we mean by training pulse rate or cardiorespiratory system, go back to "Designing Your Personalized Program."

Another item to remember applies specifically to many HYDROROBICS exercises but also concerns your exercise workout as a whole. There are different types of stretching activities that are part of "hydro." Use of stretching can prevent exercise injuries and will minimize exercise discomfort.

The two basic types of stretching are *static stretching* and *ballistic stretching*, and it's important to know how to use each type.

Static stretching is the slow and steady stretch of a muscle in the full range of motion. You'll find this kind of stretch used in the opening of several "hydro" exercises (*Flamingo, Hip Dip* and others) before you go into the dynamic motion of the exercise. Whenever you "hold" a position, you are in the static stretch.

The forceful movement that stretches the muscles explosively or dynamically is the ballistic stretch. Getting back to the *Hip Dip*, as you leave the static hold and go into the dip and arch motion, you are stretching (or should be if you're working at it) ballistically.

For more on stretching as a part of your total HYDROROBICS workout, refer to the chapter, "Designing Your Personalized Program."

Hang On

The last information you need before getting into the exercises is how to stabilize yourself either standing in the water or holding on to the side of the pool.

There are right and wrong ways to stabilize. This happens to be one of the few instructions we will give you where the right way is also the easy way. We even give you some choices on this one. Your selection of methods will be determined partly by what is most comfortable for you and, when the hand or arm is stabilizing, on the type of pool you are using.

With that, you are ready to begin HYDROROBICS. We think you will love it!

Stabilizing positions using the pool wall.

Different types of pool walls will determine the type of stabilization you use for HYDROROBICS exercises. One design has a "gutter rail" (see definition) used for gripping. The other basic design, commonly used in home pools, has a straight wall without a gutter rail. The straight edge may have a rounded corner suitable for gripping. If you use this type of pool and find it difficult to stabilize, you may want to try the pool ladder.

Prone

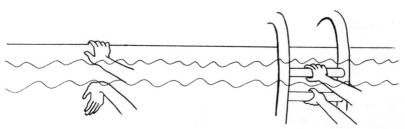

- Grip the *gutter rail* with one hand and place the palm of the other hand flat on the wall with fingers pointing downward. The bottom hand should be about 16″ below the gripping hand. Press inward with the bottom hand and pull outward with the grip hand until your body rises to the horizontal position.
- Same as above except you will grip the *edge of the pool wall* instead of a gutter rail.
- Same as for gutter rail except you will grip two rungs of the ladder. Place your hands in position on the *ladder*, one or two rungs apart.

Supine

- Reach over your shoulders and grip the *gutter rail* with both hands as you press your shoulders against the pool wall.
- Extend your arms out to the side and grip the *edge of the pool wall*.
- Reach over your shoulders and grip the sides of the *ladder*.

Standing positions for upper body exercises.

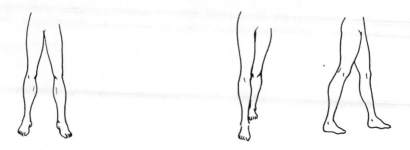

Method 1
Your feet are shoulder width apart and flat on the floor. This establishes good support for exercises that have lateral or side-to-side movement.

Method 2
Stand with one leg to the front of your body and the other to the rear of the body. Feet are flat on the pool floor. This establishes good support for exercises that have front to rear movement.
Important: All upper body exercises are done in shoulder-depth water.

Stabilization: an Exercise unto Itself

Proper stabilizing positions are important to the exercise's performance, but they are also to be considered exercises in themselves. Stabilization positions can improve your muscle tone! This is better understood when you realize that the part of the body you use for stabilizing is actually performing an isometric contraction while supporting the parts of the body being moved.

Isometric contraction is one of several methods of working your muscles for increased strength and muscle tone. Therefore, it's good to know that when doing "hydro" exercises, you're gaining benefits not only in the parts of your body that are moving dynamically, but also in the immovable parts doing the stabilizing.

6

AEROBIC EXERCISES

The foundation of any total fitness exercise program is built on the aerobic form of exercise. These exercises improve the heart's capabilities to transport much needed oxygen to the working muscles.

As you perform the *Joggernaut* or the *Cross-Country Skier*, you may be thinking about the good things you are doing for your legs and arms, but there's much more that's happening to your body in aerobic exercises.

As we explained in Chapter 2, ". . . oxygen is delivered to the muscles via the lungs and the circulatory system (including the heart) . . ." It is through aerobic exercises that we increase the efficiency of this "aerobic transport system."

Aerobic exercises are especially fun to do with another person. And if you can get a group together, the *Chorus Line* for example, is a natural for just plain grand fun.

Aerobic exercises can be performed as a special segment of your workout or as warmup to the rest of your water activities. In fact, we strongly recommend that you use one or two, such as the *Jogger-naut*, before beginning any of the other categories of exercise. (See "The Standard Workout" section.)

Remember, since the duration intervals for each fitness level are only suggestions, you may   increase or decrease the interval time as you see fit. And if the pool you are using isn't heated, you're going to love aerobics in the water. You will warm up quickly as you vigorously burn calories and increase your cardiorespiratory strength and endurance.

NOTE OF CAUTION:
If you are using an excessively warm water pool, you should limit aerobic activity to about 10 minutes, depending on your fitness level. Warm water can have a weakening effect. If you feel lightheaded or seem to be "sweating," it is time to stop any vigorous activity in the water.

BUNNY HOP (Hugh Hefner's Favorite)

BODY PARTS	FITNESS LEVEL	DURATION	SPEED
Feet, ankles,	A	2 minute-high hop	Fast
legs	B	1½ minute-medium hop	Moderate
	C	1 minute-low hop	Slow

Starting Position

Stand erect in chest-deep water with your hands on your hips or with arms crossed under the breast.

Basic Exercise

1. Keeping your knees together and slightly bent, stand on the balls of your feet.
2. Hop forward.
3. Repeating the hop-hop-hop according to your fitness level. Jumping or hopping as high as possible demands greater energy.

Variation

Perform this exercise hopping backwards.

Reminder

Don't forget to look back occasionally or beep your horn if you're not alone in the pool.

NOTE

This is a good ice-breaker for getting friends into the "hydro" routine.

CHARLESTON

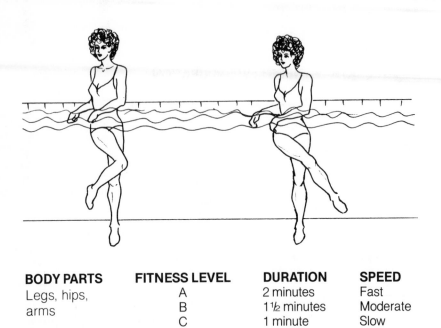

BODY PARTS	FITNESS LEVEL	DURATION	SPEED
Legs, hips, arms	A	2 minutes	Fast
	B	1½ minutes	Moderate
	C	1 minute	Slow

Starting Position

Stand erect in at least chest-deep water, feet shoulders-width apart. The position of the arms is optional: either (a) hands on hips, or (b) arms swinging opposite the kick direction as in the Charleston dance.

Basic Exercise

The following sequence is conducted in one fluid kicking motion:
1. Lift your thigh close to waist level and move it across your body.
2. Kick your leg, from the knee, twice while lowering your body (dipping motion) 3-4 inches on your supporting leg.
3. Return to the starting position.
4. Repeat movement with other leg.
5. Continue this alternating movement. Completing the kicking pattern with both legs constitutes one repetition.

Reminder

Don't perform this exercise too close to a friend! Your friendship may end up "on the limb."

CHARLESTON FLAP

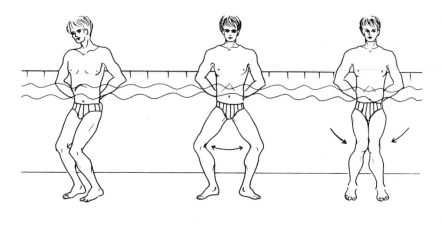

BODY PARTS	FITNESS LEVEL	DURATION	SPEED
Thigh, hips	A	2 minutes	Fast
	B	1½ minutes	Fast
	C	1 minute	Moderate

Starting Position

In waist-deep water, stand in a semi-squat position with your feet shoulders-width apart and flat on the pool floor. Place your hands on your hips.

Basic Exercise

While keeping your body in the starting position:
1. Open your knees as far apart as possible.
2. Close or flap your knees until they touch.
3. Repeat this opening and closing motion, applying equal force in both directions. The opening and closing motion constitutes one repetition.

Variation

You may vary the force by increasing the force in either the closing or opening movement while decreasing it in the opposite movement. Follow the same frequency and speed recommendations as the basic exercise.

CHEERLEADER JUMP

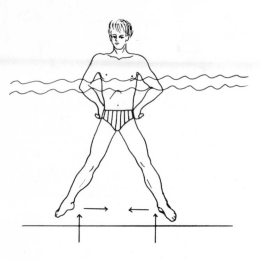

BODY PARTS	FITNESS LEVEL	DURATION	SPEED
Legs, hips, groin	A	2 minutes	Moderate
	B	1½ minutes	Moderate
	C	1 minute	Slow

Starting Position

Stand erect in shoulder-depth water and place your hands on your hips.

Basic Exercise

In one jumping movement, open and close your legs.

Reminder

Be sure to keep your legs straight.

CHORUS LINE

BODY PARTS	FITNESS LEVEL	DURATION	SPEED
Legs, hips,	A	2 minutes	Fast
stomach	B	1½ minutes	Moderate
	C	1 minute	Slow

Starting Position

Stand erect in at least waist-deep water with your feet shoulders-width apart.

Basic Exercise

The following sequence is done in one fluid kicking motion.
1. Lift your thigh to a forward, horizontal position as you hop on your supporting leg.
2. Kick your leg from the knee while again making a hopping movement with the supporting leg.
3. Return your leg to the starting position. You may add a third hopping movement at this time. Repeat this kicking and hopping movement according to your fitness level.
4. Repeat with other leg. A repetition is obtained when you've kicked once with each leg.

Variation

You can do the same exercise by performing a series of three kicks, beginning at a 45 degree angle to the left of your body, then straight ahead, finishing with a 45 degree to the right.

Reminder

If you like variety, you can start this series from the right—or make up your own variations of kick patterns. This one is more fun with one or two friends.

NOTE

Your hands may be placed on your hips or, if you're doing this exercise with a partner, placed on your partner's shoulder. You may also hold on to the side of the pool for balance.

COSSACK SHUFFLE
(Watch out Baryshnikov!)

BODY PARTS	FITNESS LEVEL	DURATION	SPEED
Legs, hips,	A	2 minutes	Fast
stomach	B	1½ minutes	Moderate
	C	1 minute	Moderate

Starting Position

Standing in shoulder-depth water, place your hands on your hips.

Basic Exercise

1. Slightly tilt your body backward.
2. Keeping legs straight, kick them forward in an alternating rhythm to an angle of about 45 degrees.

Variation

1. Instead of tilting your upper body backward, tilt it forward.
2. Perform the kick motion, or shuffle, to the rear instead of forward.
3. Hands may remain on hips, or may be straight with arms swinging in a pendulum-like motion.

Reminder

Don't forget to keep your legs straight.

CROSS COUNTRY SKIER

BODY PARTS	FITNESS LEVEL	DURATION	SPEED
Legs, hips,	A	2 minutes	Fast
shoulders, arms	B	1½ minutes	Moderate
	C	1 minute	Moderate

Starting Position

Stand erect in shoulder-depth water with arms hanging straight and palms flat.

Basic Exercise

1. We highly recommend that you look at the drawings for this one!
2. Make the jump as wide as possible.
3. Swing your arms forward and backward like a pendulum. Coordinate your arm swing with your leg movement (example: right arm—left leg forward).
4. Repeat movement according to your fitness level.

Reminder

Develop a rhythm and think "snow."

DOWNHILLER

BODY PARTS	FITNESS LEVEL	DURATION	SPEED
Feet, ankles, legs,	A	2 minutes	Fast
hips, stomach, arms,	B	1½ minutes	Moderate
shoulders	C	1 minute	Moderate

Starting Position

Stand in chest-deep water. Your arms are extended forward near the surface of the water.

Basic Exercise

1. Pretend that you are jumping from side to side over a large log that is about 15″ high.
2. As you jump, sweep both arms from side to side, opposite your jumping motion.

Reminder

Keep your legs together. Keep your arms together.

NOTE

This is an excellent pre-season exercise for skiers.

FLUTTER KICK

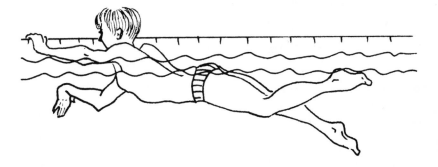

BODY PARTS	FITNESS LEVEL	DURATION	SPEED
Hips, thigh, lower leg	A	2 minutes	Fast
	B	1½ minutes	Medium
	C	1 minute	Slow

Starting Position

Place your body in a prone position, stabilizing with the method of your choice. (Of course, your face is out of the water.)

Basic Exercise

Move your legs in an alternating vertical pattern. Your feet are separating at a distance of approximately 12-15 inches. Allow your knees to bend in a continuous movement.

Variation

Turn over on your back and get a better look at the world.

THE GERBIL WHEEL
(DEDICATED TO CY TIMMONS)

Our special thanks to Cy Timmons, a well-known musician, vocalist and entertainer, who inspired this exercise with his original composition about a gerbil.

BODY PARTS	FITNESS LEVEL	DURATION	SPEED
Arms, legs	A	2 minutes	Fast
	B	1½ minutes	Moderate
	C	1 minute	Slow

Starting Position

Stand erect in shoulder-deep water with your arms at right angles in front of your body just beneath the surface of the water.

Basic Exercise

1. Run in place and lift your knees as high as possible (as in the *Joggernaut*).
2. Maintain a circular movement with your arms in front of your body.
3. Reverse the direction of the arm circles periodically.

NOTE

Cy Timmons suggests that you wiggle your nose and mouth for the full effect of this exercise.

HEEL SLAP

BODY PARTS	FITNESS LEVEL	DURATION	SPEED
Thigh, lower leg, arms	A	2 minutes	Fast
	B	1½ minutes	Moderate
	C	1 minute	Slow

Starting Position

Stand erect in chest-deep water with your hands at your sides.

Basic Exercise

1. While bending at the knee, kick your lower leg backwards and to the side high enough to meet your hand.
2. Slap the bottom of your foot with the hand.
3. Shift your weight to the leg you have just slapped and slap the other foot with the other hand.
4. Try not to get slap happy as you increase the speed of the movements according to your fitness.

Variation

Slap the right foot with the left hand, etc.

HIGH JUMP

BODY PARTS	FITNESS LEVEL	DURATION	SPEED
Feet, legs, waist,	A	2 minutes	Fast
stomach, arms	B	1½ minutes	Moderate
	C	1 minute	Slow

Starting Position

Stand erect in chest-deep water with your arms extended to the side at water level.

Basic Exercise

1. While pressing your arms downward, jump up, forcefully bending your legs toward your chest.
2. Return to starting position (as if you didn't know!).

Reminder

Keep your arms straight during this exercise. During the jump, push off from the balls of your feet.

JOGGERNAUT
(Do this with overpowering force.)

BODY PARTS	FITNESS LEVEL	DURATION	SPEED
Arms and lower	A	2½ minutes	Fast
body	B	2 minutes	Moderate
	C	1½ minutes	Moderate

Starting Position

Stand erect in chest-deep water with your arms in a jogger's position (forearms directed forward at a right angle to the upper arm).

Basic Exercise

1. Run in place and lift your knees up as high as possible for extra stretch.
2. Swing your arms in an alternating forward motion as you jog.

Reminder

This is an excellent first exercise for warming up.

Variation #1

Jog in an actual run the width of your pool.

Variation #2

On the lifting motion of the knee, angle the knee as high as possible to the side instead of to the front of the body.

JUMPING JACKS

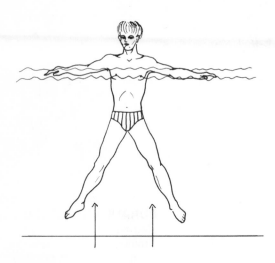

BODY PARTS	FITNESS LEVEL	DURATION	SPEED
Arms, groin, legs,	A	2 minutes	Fast
feet	B	1½ minutes	Moderate
	C	1 minute	Slow

Starting Position

For the two-count two-step jumping jack, stand erect in shoulder-depth water with arms to the side of the body.

Basic Exercise

1. While keeping arms and legs straight, forcefully jump as wide as possible to an open leg position.
2. Swing your arms to the side of your body up to the water level.
3. Arm and leg movements should be coordinated.
4. Jump back to the starting position, again coordinating the movements of the arms and legs.

Variation

Move your legs apart half the distance and increase the speed.

ONE LEG HOP

BODY PARTS	FITNESS LEVEL	DURATION	SPEED
Feet, legs	A	1½ minutes	Moderate
	B	1 minute	Moderate
	C	1 minute	Slow

Starting Position

Stand in chest-deep water on one foot with leg straight. Lift the other leg to your chest while bending the leg at the knee. For added balance, grip the bent leg with your hands and hold it against your body.

Basic Exercise

1. Hop on the supporting leg repeatedly, 4-5 times or until that leg gets tired.
2. Alternate to the other leg in the same position.

Reminder

The hopping should be done on the balls of the feet.

Variation

Vary your hopping motion by alternating a springing hop and a short hop.

POLARIS
(hop)

BODY PARTS	FITNESS LEVEL	DURATION	SPEED
Feet, ankles,	A	2 minutes	Moderate
legs	B	1½ minutes	Moderate
	C	1 minute	Slow

Starting Position

Stand in chest-deep water in an upright position with feet shoulders-width apart and hands placed on hips.

Basic Exercise

1. Squat to neck-deep water. With an explosive movement, jump as high out of the water as possible, like a missile. During the jump be sure to push off the balls of your feet.
2. Return to the squatting position and repeat the jumping movement.

Reminder

The arms are in the hands-on-hips position in order to create greater resistance.

Variation

Vary your jumping motion by alternating a short hop with the jump.

SCISSORS JUMP

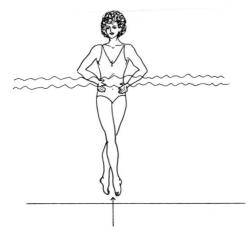

BODY PARTS	FITNESS LEVEL	DURATION	SPEED
Legs	A	2 minutes	Moderate
	B	1½ minutes	Moderate
	C	1 minute	Slow

Starting Position

Stand erect in chest-deep water with your hands on your hips.

Basic Exercise

1. Jump as high as you can while crossing your legs. Keep your legs straight.
2. Jump up again and reverse the cross.

Variation

Keeping them straight, cross your arms in a synchronized motion with the legs.

SIDE LEG SIDE

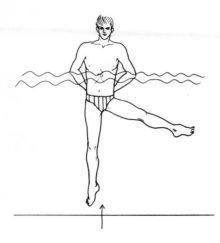

BODY PARTS	FITNESS LEVEL	DURATION	SPEED
Legs, groin	A	2 minutes	Moderate
	B	1½ minutes	Moderate
	C	1 minute	Fast

Starting Position

Stand erect in shoulder-depth water with hands on hips.

Basic Exercise

1. Swing one leg out to your side as high as possible while hopping twice on the other leg.
2. Return swinging leg to supporting position and, in a continuous motion, repeat movements with other leg in opposite direction.
3. Develop a rhythm according to your fitness level.

7

Lower Body Exercises

These exercises are second only to middle body exercises in popularity. Almost everyone thinks they could use some improvement in the legs or hips or buttocks (too big or too flat or too flabby or too something). Remember, this part of the body supports all the weight of all the other parts. The lower body is also featured in the aerobic exercises that are designed to improve your cardiorespiratory fitness and endurance.

So let's give this part of the body all the help we can. At this point, you'll be working on flexibility and body contouring. Some of the exercises will seem simple and straightforward; a few are a bit more complicated. And some will inspire you to bring a radio or phonograph to the pool. You might even want to invite a few friends to do the *Flamingo* with you.

Whether your workout concentrates on one part of the body at a time or includes a mix of exercises, we know you are going to enjoy the improvements in the lower body.

Be sure to do all the exercises in at least waist-deep water.

Here's to smaller or fuller or tighter or whatever! Get going!

NOTE:
When the variation of the basic exercise indicates that you should speed up the movement, you should also double the number of repetitions suggested in the *frequency* (Do not double the *duration* times).

ANKLE ACTION

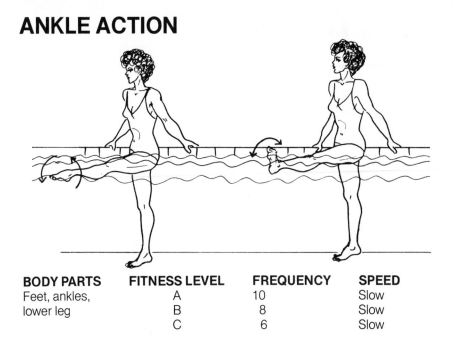

BODY PARTS	FITNESS LEVEL	FREQUENCY	SPEED
Feet, ankles,	A	10	Slow
lower leg	B	8	Slow
	C	6	Slow

Starting Position

Standing with your back to the wall, stabilize your upper body using the method of your choice. Raise one leg in front to a 45 degree position. Keep your supporting leg straight with the foot flat on the floor.

Basic Exercise

1. Keeping your leg straight, rotate the foot about the ankle in a counterclockwise circular motion.
2. Repeat in a clockwise direction.
3. Repeat the clockwise/counterclockwise sequence with the other foot.

Variation

1. Point or extend the toes forward and hold for 8 seconds.
2. Flex or point your toes back toward your body for 8 seconds or longer. Repeat this combination and do five repititions.
3. Repeat the extend-and-flex sequence with your other leg.

Warning

If you are getting foot cramps on the extend or flex, you're using too much force. Take it easy!

CALF BUILDER

BODY PARTS	FITNESS LEVEL	FREQUENCY	SPEED
Lower leg	A	4	Slow
	B	4	Slow
	C	4	Slow

Starting Position

Face the side of the pool and stabilize your body by extending your arms forward and gripping a portion of the pool wall. Your feet must be flat on the pool floor.

Basic Exercise

1. Raise your heels as far off the floor as possible while balancing on your toes.
2. Hold this static stretch position for an 8-second count or longer.
3. Return to the starting position and repeat.

Variation

For endurance, repeat the basic exercise with a continuous up and down, bouncing-like movement for approximately one-half minute.

FLAMINGO

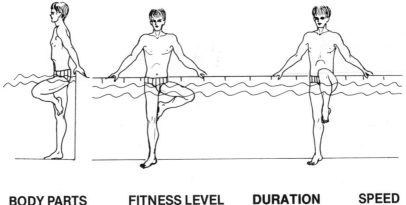

BODY PARTS	FITNESS LEVEL	DURATION	SPEED
Groin, upper leg	A	2 minutes	Slow
	B	1½ minutes	Slow
	C	1 minute	Slow

Starting Position

Standing with your back to the wall, stabilize the body with the method of your choice. While lifting and bending one leg, place the bottom of the heel against the inner thigh (near knee) of your supporting leg. Your buttocks should be against the wall.

Basic Exercise

1. Keep the bent leg as close to the wall as possible.
2. Keep your heel fixed in this position and swing your knee as far to the left and back as far to the right as possible. If you are extremely flexible in the groin area, you may be able to touch the wall on the swing. Repeat.
3. Repeat with the other leg.

Variation

Halve the distance of the swing and pick up the speed.

Reminder

This won't be easy!! But try to keep your buttocks and lower back to the wall during this exercise.

HALF MOON

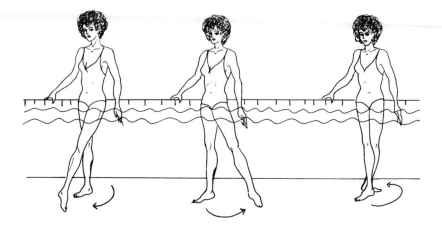

BODY PARTS	FITNESS LEVEL	FREQUENCY	SPEED
Groin, hips,	A	16	Fast
thigh	B	12	Moderate
	C	10	Slow

Starting Position

Stand with the side of your body 90 degrees to the pool wall. Secure your position (no more than one foot from the wall) by gripping the pool wall with your hand.

Basic Exercise

1. Keeping your leg straight, move the outer leg forward and inward until your inner ankle touches the side of the pool. Your supporting leg remains straight and motionless.
2. While moving in a "C"-like pattern, extend the leg from the forward to a backward position behind the supporting leg. The inner ankle should once again touch the side of the pool.
3. Repeat this forward to backward "C"-like movement with equal force in both directions.
4. Reverse body position and repeat exercise with other leg.

LATERAL LIFT

BODY PARTS	FITNESS LEVEL	FREQUENCY	SPEED
Hips, groin, thigh	A	12	Moderate
	B	10	Slow
	C	8	Slow

Starting Position

Stand erect with your body facing 90 degrees away from the side of the pool. Stabilize your body by extending one arm to grip the pool wall.

Basic Exercise

1. Lift your outer leg as high as possible laterally (to the side) but not above the level of the water.
2. Lower the leg downward and across the *front* of the supporting leg as far as possible.
3. Repeat the lift motion as in #1. This time lower the leg downward and across the *back* of the supporting leg. Don't be surprised if your leg cannot reach as far as the pool wall.
4. Repeat with equal force in both directions.
5. Reverse body position and repeat exercise with other leg.

Variation

1. Lift the leg only half the distance but increase the speed. This is especially good for the thigh muscles.
2. Maximize the force of movement in either the upward or downward direction while decreasing the force in the opposite direction.

Reminder

Keep your leg straight throughout the full range of motion. Keep your upper body from tilting.

LEFT-RIGHT-LEFT

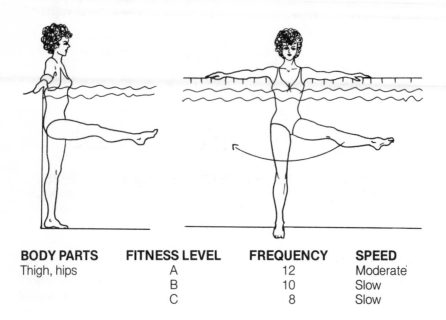

BODY PARTS	FITNESS LEVEL	FREQUENCY	SPEED
Thigh, hips	A	12	Moderate
	B	10	Slow
	C	8	Slow

Starting Position

Standing with your back to the wall, stabilize your upper body by the method of your choice. Raise one leg in front to a 45 degree position with your foot semiflexed. (This will help prevent cramping of the foot muscles). Keep supporting leg straight with foot flat on the pool floor.

Basic Exercise

While keeping your leg straight, move the leg left to right as far as possible.

Variation

Shorten the distance of the movement by at least half and increase the speed of movement.

Reminder

It is important to keep your leg straight in order to have your thigh and groin benefit from the exercise. Keep your buttocks and upper body pressed to the wall.

LEG CIRCLES

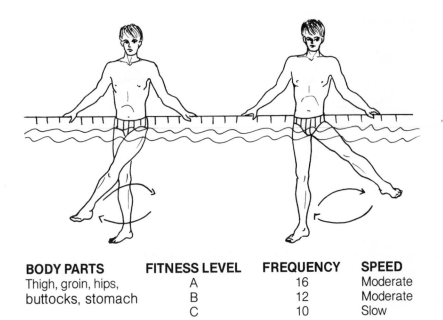

BODY PARTS	FITNESS LEVEL	FREQUENCY	SPEED
Thigh, groin, hips,	A	16	Moderate
buttocks, stomach	B	12	Moderate
	C	10	Slow

Starting Position

Standing with your back to the wall, stabilize the upper body using the method of your choice. Raise one leg in front to a 45 degree position with your foot semiflexed. (This will help prevent cramping of the foot muscles.) Keep supporting leg straight with foot flat on the pool floor.

Basic Exercise

1. With leg straight, begin a clockwise circular motion. The circular pattern being made by the foot should be at least 24″ in diameter. Repeat.
2. Repeat movement in counterclockwise direction.
3. Repeat #1 and #2 with other leg.

Reminder

Keep your buttocks pressed to the wall and legs straight.

Variation

Repeat above exercise with a smaller motion (6 to 8″). Increase the speed of the circular movement.

LEG STRETCH

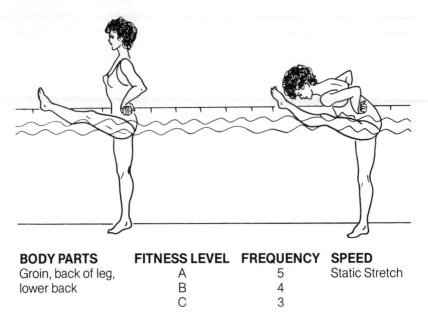

BODY PARTS	FITNESS LEVEL	FREQUENCY	SPEED
Groin, back of leg,	A	5	Static Stretch
lower back	B	4	
	C	3	

Starting Position

Face the side of the pool approximately a leg's distance from the pool wall. Lift one leg forward and fix or hook your foot to some object on the edge of the pool (gutter rail, ladder, etc.).

Basic Exercise

1. For your first "hurdle," try to slowly straighten your leg. You are allowed to yell "ouch"—or worse. Hold this stretch position for 6-8 seconds.
2. Repeat.
3. If you managed to perform #1 above, lean forward over your leg with the upper body. Hold this position for 6-8 seconds and repeat.
4. Repeat with the other leg.

Reminder

Before doing this exercise, check Chapter 5 for more on flexibility.

NOTE

If have exceptional flexibility, (or a big nose) you may be able to touch your nose to your kneecap. You're in the big time now!!

PENDULUM

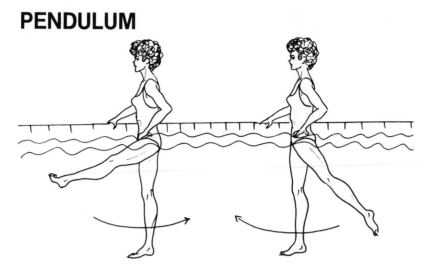

BODY PARTS	FITNESS LEVEL	FREQUENCY	SPEED
Legs, hip joint,	A	12	Moderate
stomach, buttocks	B	10	Slow
	C	8	Slow

Starting Position

Stand with the side of your body 90 degrees to the pool wall. Extend your arm and grip the pool wall.

Basic Exercise

1. While keeping your outer leg straight, move it forward (from the hip) and as far upward as your muscles will permit.
2. Still working from the hip joint, swing your leg from a forward to backward position, extending the leg as far backward as possible.
3. Repeat this forward and backward swinging motion with equal force.
4. Reverse body position and repeat exercise with outer leg.

Variation

Increase the speed of movement, but only move the leg one-half the distance forward and backward.

Reminders

Keep your leg straight throughout the full range of motion. Move the leg in a vertical pattern. Keep your upper body from tilting forward or backward.

PLIÉ

BODY PARTS	FITNESS LEVEL	FREQUENCY	SPEED
Legs, groin	A	16	Moderate
	B	12	Moderate
	C	10	Slow

Starting Position

Stand erect in waist deep water with hands on hips, heels together, and feet at a 45 degree angle (like a duck!).

Basic Exercise

1. Lower your body by bending the knees to a squatting position, about 12″ or until the upper and lower legs form a right angle. If your head is under the water you did not follow these instructions. Seek higher ground.
2. Return to starting position.
3. Repeat.

Reminder

Try this one to "Swan Lake" or other appropriate music.

QUAD STRETCH

BODY PARTS	FITNESS LEVEL	FREQUENCY	SPEED
Upper leg,	A	10	Moderate
buttocks, lower	B	7	Moderate
back	C	5	Slow

Starting Position

Face the wall with both feet flat on the floor and extend your arms forward to grip the wall.

Basic Exercise

1. Initiate a backward kicking (lifting) motion, allowing your lower leg to bend at the knee and swing upwards.
2. Repeat.
3. Repeat exercise with other leg.

Warning

Go slowly at first. If you have a lower back problem , take it easy with this one or don't do it at all.

NOTE

Your upper leg moves slightly backwards from the hip joint.

SCISSORS CROSS

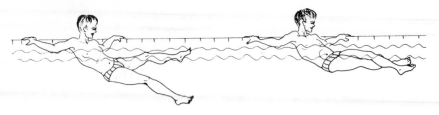

BODY PARTS	FITNESS LEVEL	FREQUENCY	SPEED
Hips, thighs	A	20	Moderate
	B	16	Moderate
	C	12	Slow

Starting Position

Raise your body to a supine (face up) position in the water with your head toward the wall. Stabilize by the method of your choice. Your legs should be together and straight.

Basic Exercise

1. Open your legs simultaneously as far apart as possible; do not bend your knees.
2. Close your legs simultaneously, allowing them to cross as far as possible.
3. Repeat the leg movement to an open position.
4. Repeat the closing/crossing movement with your legs in reverse position.
5. Repeat according to the frequency for your fitness level.

Variation

Perform the exercise in the same manner as above except open your legs half the distance and increase the speed.

Reminder

If your bottom is sinking (which has been know to happen), try another method of stabilizing your upper body.

SWIFT KICK

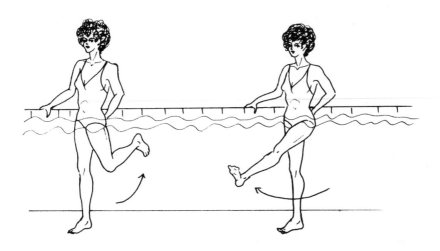

BODY PARTS	FITNESS LEVEL	FREQUENCY	SPEED
Stomach, hips,	A	12	Fast
buttocks, legs	B	10	Moderate
	C	8	Slow

Starting Position

Stand erect with your body facing 90 degrees away from the side of the pool. Secure your position by extending your arm in order to grip the pool wall.

Basic Exercise

1. Lift your outer leg upward and behind your body in a kicking position with the knee bent. Balance yourself on your supporting leg, assisted with the hand grip on the pool wall. You are now in the "pre-kick" or "set" position.
2. Execute a football-like kicking motion from the hip and knee joint, moving the leg forward through the full range of motion. At the end of the kicking movement your leg will be fully straight and near the surface of the water (if you are reasonably flexible).
3. Return the leg slowly to the kicking "set" position.
4. Repeat the kick.
5. Reverse body position and repeat the kicking series with the other leg.

WIDE LEG KICK

BODY PARTS	FITNESS LEVEL	DURATION	SPEED
Groin, hips,	A	3 minutes	Moderate
buttocks, legs	B	2 minutes	Moderate
	C	1½ minutes	Slow

Starting Position

Stabilize your body in a prone position by the method of your choice.

Basic Exercise

Keeping your legs straight, move your legs apart in an exaggerated flutter kick motion. The legs should separate as far apart as possible, with the lower leg almost touching the bottom of the pool. Your feet should never break the surface of the water. Remember, do not bend your knees!

Variation

Repeat the above exercise, moving your legs approximately half the distance while increasing the speed. Continue keeping your legs straight. This variation, performed for at least 1-3 minutes, develops muscle endurance.

Reminder

This one might get boring—so keep a radio tuned to your favorite station and kick to the music!!

8

Middle Body Exercises

If you are the rare and perfect specimen who does not need to exercise an embarrassing (in your opinion) part of the middle body, then you may pass up this section of exercises. Of course, if you are satisfied with the firm condition of your mid body, you'll want to keep it that way. You'd better read on. We think you will be especially pleased with this group of exercises. We concentrate on the abdomen, hips, lower back and waist area. We will be stretching, tightening and contouring.

You can notice a measurable difference in this part of your body, *if* you do the exercises regularly and correctly over a period of weeks. It is through repeated performance of such exercises as the *Six-Count Twister* and the *Hula Hoop* that you may see a change in clothing size.

Some people also think that these are the most creative and attractive of the HYDROROBICS groups. The almost ballet-like movement of the *Hip Dip* or the karate action that begins in *Fire Hydrant* are just a few of the innovative routines you'll perform as you improve your middle body.

And let's not ignore the source of chronic pain that can affect the entire body, the lower back. Strengthening this critical area can reduce or eliminate problems caused by poor posture, weak muscles and tension. And very few of you can admit to never having experienced tension!

As we've mentioned elsewhere, the mid body exercises are the most popular, and most people consider at least one of them to be their favorite. Whatever your reason for exercising, the middle body will be a focal point in your HYDROROBICS workout.

NOTE:
When the variation of the basic exercise indicates that you should speed up the movement, you should also double the number of repetitions suggested in the *frequency* (do not double *duration* times).

BODY TWIST

BODY PARTS	FITNESS LEVEL	FREQUENCY	SPEED
Shoulders,	A	10	Slow
torso	B	8	Slow
	C	6	Slow

Starting Position

Stand in chest-deep water with your back to the wall. Extend your arms behind you and grip the wall with both hands.

Basic Exercise

1. Make a series of small steps that twist your lower body to the left. Your upper body should be facing forward.
2. Now make a 180 degree turn to the right with small steps.
3. Continue this twisting movement, going from side to side.

Variation

Instead of using small steps, jump from side to side, keeping upper body stable.

DOUBLE LEG LIFT

BODY PARTS	FITNESS LEVEL	FREQUENCY	SPEED
Shoulders, arms	A	12	Fast
back, stomach,	B	10	Moderate
hips	C	8	Moderate

Starting Position

Stand erect in chest-deep water with your back to the wall and secure a grip with your arms on the edge of the pool.

Basic Exercise

1. Brace your back against the wall and lift both of your legs briskly upward.
2. Keep your legs straight and try to lift your legs to the surface of the water.
3. Pull your knees to your chest.
4. Forcefully lower your legs to the starting position.
5. Repeat.

Reminder

Keep your back flat against the wall.

FIRE HYDRANT

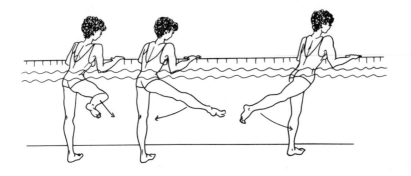

BODY PARTS	FITNESS LEVEL	FREQUENCY	SPEED
Hips, groin, legs	A	10	Moderate
	B	8	Moderate
	C	6	Slow

Starting Position

Standing in chest-deep water and facing the wall, stabilize your upper body with both feet flat on the floor. Extend your arms forward and grip the wall. Your upper body should be tilted slightly forward.

Basic Exercise

1. Lift one leg as high as possible to the side with the knee bent.
2. In a forceful kicking motion, straighten your leg (similar to a karate side kick).
3. In a sweeping motion, thrust your leg to a position directly behind you.
   NOTE: During this movement your pelvic axis has shifted from a tilted to a flat position in the water.
4. Now lower your leg with force to the starting position.
5. Repeat with suggested frequency.
6. Repeat exercise with the other leg.

Variation

You may alternate from one leg to the other instead of the pattern above.

HIP DIP

BODY PARTS	FITNESS LEVEL	FREQUENCY	SPEED
Upper torso,	A	12	Slow
hips	B	10	Slow
	C	10	Slow

Starting Position

Stand in chest-deep water and position your body perpendicular to the wall. Extend your inside arm (straight) and take a grip on the wall. Now take a short side step away from the wall so that you are on a slant.

Basic Exercise

1. Keep your gripping arm straight as you dip your hip as close as possible toward the wall. Hold for a ten second stretch.
2. Now extend your hip as far away from the wall as possible and arch your outer arm over your head. Hold this position for ten seconds.
3. Alternate these two movements in a continuous rhythmic motion.
4. Turn around and repeat the exercise in the other direction.

Reminder

Both your feet should remain flat on the floor for maximum stretch effect.

NOTE

Master this and you're ready for Hawaiian hula dancing.

HULA HOOP

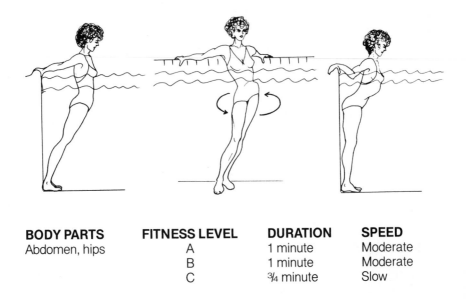

BODY PARTS	FITNESS LEVEL	DURATION	SPEED
Abdomen, hips	A	1 minute	Moderate
	B	1 minute	Moderate
	C	¾ minute	Slow

Starting Position

Stand erect in shoulder depth water with your back to the wall. Grip the wall behind you with both hands approximately shoulder-width apart. Your arms are straight and the heels of your feet should be touching the base of the wall.

Basic Exercise

1. a. Arch your back and extend your stomach as far forward as possible.
   b. Bend at the waist until your buttocks touch the wall.
   c. Repeat this swaying motion.
2. a. Make a circular motion with your hips, extending them as far as possible in all directions. Be sure that your upper body remains stable as you rotate your lower body.
   b. As you maintain this continuous fluid motion, don't forget to reverse the direction of your circle every 3 to 4 revolutions.

LEAP FROG

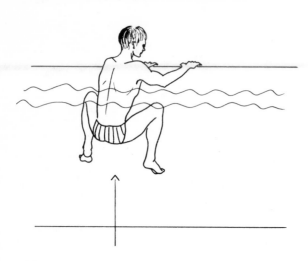

BODY PARTS	FITNESS LEVEL	FREQUENCY	SPEED
Stomach,	A	15	Moderate
lower body	B	12	Moderate
	C	8	Slow

Starting Position

Stand erect in shoulder-depth water facing the wall. Extend your arms and grip the wall with both hands (approximately shoulders-width apart).

Basic Exercise

1. Leap up forcefully with your knees extended to the outside of your arms. Your knees will break the surface of the water and be sharply angled.
2. Return to the starting position and repeat the leaping movement.

Reminder

On the uplifting movement, make a croaking sound (optional).

NOTE

You should be working on the balls of your feet, not flat-footed.

MODIFIED SCISSORS CROSS

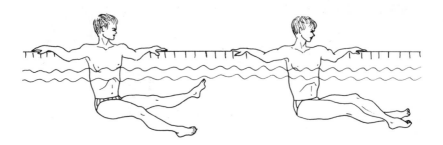

BODY PARTS	FITNESS LEVEL	FREQUENCY	SPEED
Upper body,	A	16	Moderate
stomach, legs	B	14	Moderate
	C	12	Slow

Starting Position

Stand erect in chest-deep water with your back to the wall and secure a grip with your arms on the side of the pool.

Basic Exercise

1. Brace your back against the wall and lift both your legs upward to form a right angle with your body.
2. Open your legs as far as possible.
3. Close your legs in a cross position.
4. Open your legs again.
5. Repeat with a criss-cross movement.

Variation

Shorten the distance and increase the speed for greater endurance.

SIX COUNT TWISTER

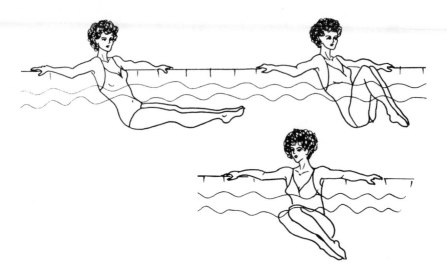

BODY PARTS	FITNESS LEVEL	FREQUENCY	SPEED
Shoulders, arms	A	16	Moderate
torso, hips	B	12	Moderate
	C	10	Slow

Starting Position

Stabilize your body in a supine position by the method of your choice. Legs should be straight and feet together.

Basic Exercise

1. Keeping your legs together, bring your knees up to your chest.
2. Twist your legs to the left.
3. Twist your legs 180 degrees to the right.
4. Repeat #2 and #3 one more time.
5. Straighten out your legs to the starting position for a count of six.

NOTE

Since you will be twisting your mid body, it's important to firmly stabilize your arms and shoulders against the pool wall.

WINDSHIELD WIPER

BODY PARTS	FITNESS LEVEL	FREQUENCY	SPEED
Shoulders, arms	A	10	Moderate
torso, stomach,	B	8	Slow
hips, thigh	C	6	Slow

Starting Position

Stand erect in chest-deep water with your back to the wall and secure a grip with your arms on the side of the pool.

Basic Exercise

1. Brace your back against the wall and lift both your legs upward to form a right angle with your body.
2. In a sweeping motion swing both your legs as far to the left as possible. Hold in this position for ten seconds.
3. Now, swing your legs as far to the right as possible and again hold for ten seconds.
4. Eliminate the static stretch (10 second hold) and move continuously from left to right (dynamic movement).

Variation

For greater endurance, shorten the distance and increase the speed.

NOTE

Remember that your back should be as flat against the wall as possible.

Women in particular have a special need to exercise their upper body.

9

Upper Body Exercises

Why?—you ask—should I bother to exercise my upper body? Women in particular tend to neglect the upper body muscles when they think about exercise. They are frequently more concerned with lower body and mid section problems. But, women in particular have a *special need* for exercising such body parts as arms, shoulders, back, chest and neck.

We've already mentioned the flab that seems to suddenly appear on the upper arm where we hadn't expected to see it. Male or female—if a muscle isn't used, it will lose it's tone and strength. Many of the exercises in this section will utilize those arm muscles.

And don't forget the muscles that support the breast area—the back, shoulders and chest. "Hydro" won't increase or reduce breast size, but it will strengthen some of those surrounding and supporting muscles. That means a benefit to breasts of any size.

Another very special reason for exercising the upper body is that feeling of relaxation following a workout that includes neck and shoulder exercises. If you've ever experienced a neck and shoulder massage, you know the feeling. Upper body tension can be reduced with some of the special exercises you'll find in this section. Be sure to perform all of these exercises in *shoulder depth water*.

NOTE:
When the variation of the basic exercise indicates you should speed up the movement, you should also double the number of repetitions suggested in the *frequency* (Do not double *duration* times).

You may want to begin or end your exercise with the upper body.

AGITATOR

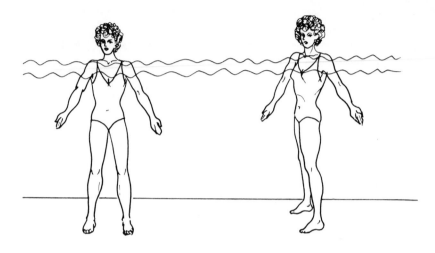

BODY PARTS	FITNESS LEVEL	DURATION	SPEED
Shoulders, arms, torso	A	2 minutes	Moderate
	B	1½ minutes	Moderate
	C	1 minute	Slow

Starting Position

Stabilize your body by method #1 in shoulder-depth water. Your arms are straight and at a 45 degree angle from your side. Your palms are facing forward with fingers together.

Basic Exercise

Twist your upper body from side to side in an agitator-like motion. Keep your arms fixed in the starting position. The entire upper body moves as a unit—just like the "agitator" in a washing machine.

Variation

Place your hands on your hips and position your elbows away from the sides of your body. Now, agitate!

ARM CIRCLES

BODY PARTS	FITNESS LEVEL	DURATION	SPEED
Neck, shoulders	A	1 minute	Moderate
	B	¾ minute	Moderate
	C	½ minute	Slow

Starting Position

Stabilize your body by method #1. Extend your arms straight out on each side at a 45 degree angle. Your hands are in a vertical "thumbs up" position.

Basic Exercise

1. Rotate your arms in a large circular motion (approximately one and one half feet in diameter).
2. Change the direction of the circle every 4-5 revolutions.

Variations

1. Repeat the basic exercise but rotate the position of the hand so that the palms face a backward "thumbs down" position. This change works the arm muscles at a different angle.
2. Make smaller circles (approximately 6 inches in diameter) and increase the speed.
3. Extend the arms to the front of the body and perform the same exercises as above.

ARM PENDULUM

BODY PARTS	FITNESS LEVEL	FREQUENCY	SPEED
Neck, shoulders	A	12	Moderate
	B	10	Slow
	C	8	Slow

Starting Position

Stabilize your body by method #2. Arms are hanging at your sides with palms facing behind you.

Basic Exercise

In a sweeping, pendulum-like motion, thrust your arms as far forward and as far backward as possible. Keep your arms straight.

Variation

Reverse the direction of your palms. This direction change will work the arm muscles a little differently. You *will* feel a difference.

DOUBLE ARM LIFT AND PRESS

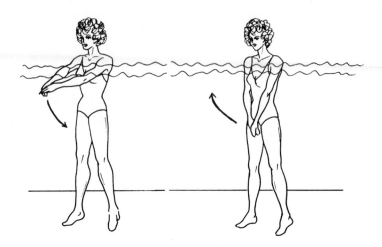

BODY PARTS	FITNESS LEVEL	FREQUENCY	SPEED
Arms, shoulders,	A	20	Moderate
chest	B	16	Moderate
	C	12	Slow

Starting Position

Stabilize your body by method # 1. Extend your arms in front of your body. Your hands are joined in a palms-down position.

Basic Exercise

1. Forcefully press your arms downward toward your groin.
2. Return arms to starting position with equal force in a sweeping motion.

Variations

1. Reduce distance of motion and increase speed.
2. Perform the same movements as in the basic exercise but behind your back.

Warning

You will have the tendency to lean forward with the upper body on the downward motion. Don't do it!!

FIGURE EIGHT

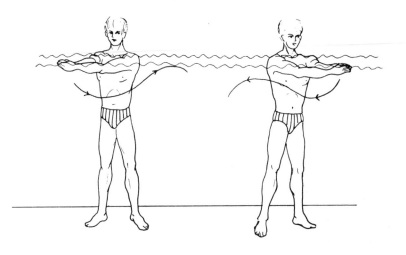

BODY PARTS	FITNESS LEVEL	FREQUENCY	SPEED
Arms, chest,	A	16	Moderate
upper body	B	12	Moderate
	C	10	Slow

Starting Position

Stabilize your body by method #1. Extend your arms with palms touching each other just beneath the surface of the water.

Basic Exercise

1. Trace a large figure 8 in the water in front of your upper body. Your arms should be straight, and all movement should originate from the shoulder area.
2. Reverse direction of the pattern.

Variation

Reduce size of figure 8 and increase speed of motion.

FIGUREHEAD

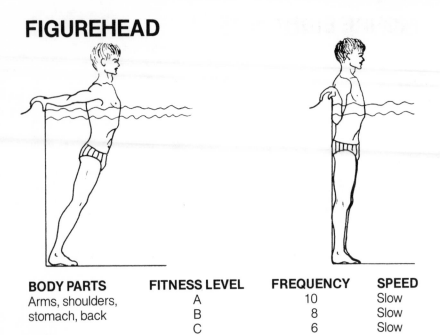

BODY PARTS	FITNESS LEVEL	FREQUENCY	SPEED
Arms, shoulders,	A	10	Slow
stomach, back	B	8	Slow
	C	6	Slow

Starting Position

Stand erect in shoulder-depth water with your back to the wall. Grip the wall behind you with both hands somewhat more than shoulder-width apart. Your arms are straight and the heels of your feet should be touching the base of the wall.

Basic Exercise

1. Arch your back and extend your stomach as far forward as possible.
2. Hold this position for about 8 seconds or longer (static stretch).
3. While dropping your elbows, pull your body backward. Stop when your back is pressed against the wall, and once again hold for 8 seconds.
4. Eliminate the 8-second holding position and repeat according to your fitness level.

Warning

Move *slowly* into the arch position. Eliminate this exercise if you have any serious back problems or feel extreme pain.

NOTE

The success of this exercise depends on the distance of the hand grips. Experiment to find what's right for you.

GOLF SWING

BODY PARTS	FITNESS LEVEL	FREQUENCY	SPEED
Shoulders,	A	16	Moderate
back	B	12	Moderate
	C	10	Slow

Starting Position

Stabilize your body by method #1. Extend arms downward in front of the body with palms touching. Lean slightly foward from the waist.

Basic Exercise

1. Swing your arms to one side of the body and up as high as possible.
2. Reverse the motion to the opposite side of the body.
3. This left-to-right motion should be done in a vertical plane.

Variation

Shorten the distance of the swing motion and speed up the movement.

NOTE

If you get a hole in one, let us know!

MAE WEST

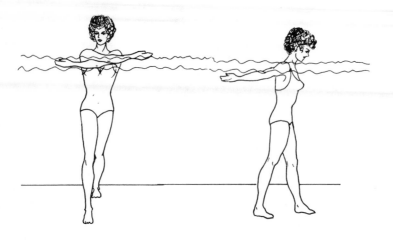

BODY PARTS	FITNESS LEVEL	FREQUENCY	SPEED
Neck, shoulders,	A	12	Moderate
chest, upper	B	10	Moderate
back	C	8	Slow

Starting Position

Stabilize your body by method #2. Extend straight arms in a crossed position in front of the body. Your hands are in a vertical, "thumbs up" position. Perform in shoulder-depth water.

Basic Exercise

1. In a sweeping motion, swing your arms behind you as far as possible. The higher your arms are angled during this motion, the more effective the exercise.
2. In a sweeping forward motion, thrust the arms back to the starting position.

Variation

Decrease the size of the sweeping movement by one half and increase the speed. This eliminates the crossing of the arms in front of the body.

Reminder

Maintain open palms to the direction of the movement at all times.

QUACK, QUACK

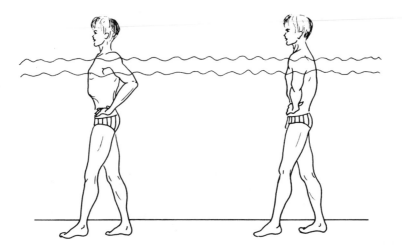

BODY PARTS	FITNESS LEVEL	FREQUENCY	SPEED
Neck, shoulders,	A	14	Moderate
chest, upper	B	12	Moderate
back	C	10	Slow

Starting Position

Stabilize your body with method #2. Place hands on hips. Perform in shoulder-depth water.

Basic Exercise

Flap your elbows in a forward to backward motion, while keeping your hands firmly on your hips.

NOTE

If you feel "fowl," quack.

SHAKE (it out)!

For "upper body therapy," relax your upper body and shake it.

SHOULDER SHRUG

BODY PARTS	FITNESS LEVEL	FREQUENCY	SPEED
Neck, shoulders	A	10	Moderate
	B	8	Slow
	C	8	Slow

Starting Position

Stabilize your body by method #1 in neck-deep water. Your hands should be on your hips.

Basic Exercise

1. Lift your shoulders up toward your neck as high as they will go. In a circular motion, move the shoulders forward and downward. In other words, shrug your shoulders in a continuous circular motion.
2. Reverse the direction of the shrugging motion (circle).

TIDAL WAVE

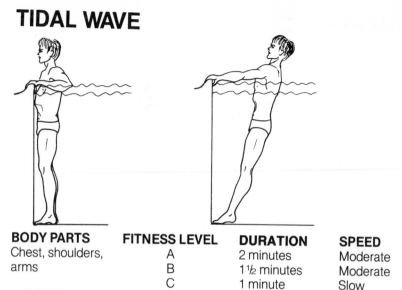

BODY PARTS	FITNESS LEVEL	DURATION	SPEED
Chest, shoulders, arms	A	2 minutes	Moderate
	B	1½ minutes	Moderate
	C	1 minute	Slow

Starting Position

Stand erect in shoulder-depth water while facing and pressing the wall. Your toes should be touching the wall. Reach up and grip the wall with both hands. Keep your elbows to your sides.

Basic Exercise

This is a two-count exercise.
1. First, keep your body straight and push yourself away from the wall.
2. Next, pull yourself in to the starting position.
3. Push and pull vigorously with equal force.
4. Repeat according to your fitness level.

Variation

1. Increase the force of push-away movement while decreasing the force of the pull-in movement.
2. Reverse of Variation #1

Reminder

Keep your mouth closed.

NOTE

This exercise used to be called the push-away, pull-away. Its name has been changed to reflect its disastrous effect.

TRAFFIC COP

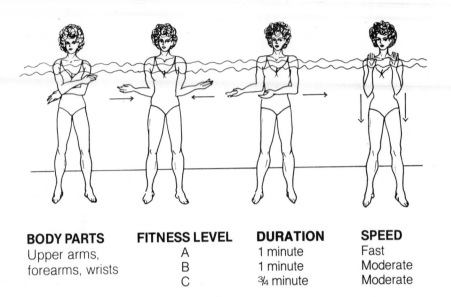

BODY PARTS	FITNESS LEVEL	DURATION	SPEED
Upper arms,	A	1 minute	Fast
forearms, wrists	B	1 minute	Moderate
	C	¾ minute	Moderate

The suggested duration applies to each of the three parts of the exercise; thus, fitness level A will do a total of 3 minutes if all parts are used.

Starting Position

Stabilize body with method #1 in shoulder-depth water. Lift your forearms in front of your body with the palms facing each other about 7 to 8 inches apart. Your elbows should be against the side of your body. Your fingers are together, providing resistance to the water.

Basic Exercise

1. a. Cross your forearms until your hands touch your elbows.
   b. Uncross your forearms in a dynamic motion.
   c. Repeat with a criss-cross movement.
2. a. While keeping hands parallel, make a left to right sweeping motion with your forearms. Your palms continue to face each other.
   b. Be sure that your fingers are still together.
3. a. Turn palms downward and move your forearms in an up and down forceful motion.

Variation

Turn palms upward in order to work the forearm muscles at a different angle.

NOTE

All action is from the elbow joint. Your upper arm stays against the body. The more force you apply to any of these movements, the greater the demand on your muscles.

WING FLAP

BODY PARTS	FITNESS LEVEL	FREQUENCY	SPEED
Neck, shoulders,	A	16	Moderate
arms	B	14	Moderate
	C	12	Slow

Starting Position

Stabilize your body by method #1. Your arms should be straight and at your side with your palms facing your body. (Like the position of "Attention!")

Basic Exercise

1. Lift your arms to a horizontal position in the water and return them to the starting position.
2. This motion is done continuously like the flapping of a bird's wings.

Variation

1. Increase the speed of the motion while decreasing the distance of the flapping movement by one-half.
2. Maximize the force of movement in either the upward or downward direction while decreasing the force in the opposite direction.

WRIST ACTION

BODY PARTS	FITNESS LEVEL	FREQUENCY	SPEED
Forearms,	A	12	Moderate
wrists	B	10	Slow
	C	10	Slow

Starting Position

Stabilize your body with method #1 in shoulder-depth water. Your elbows are at your sides as in the *Traffic Cop* exercise. Your fingers are together.

Basic Exercise

1. Without moving your forarms:
   a. Make a circular motion with your hand. Be sure to keep your fingers together.
   b. Reverse the direction of the circular movement approximately every three circles.
   c. Experiment with different combinations of direction.
2. Turn palms downward and wave "bye-bye"—forcefully. Be sure to keep your forearms in a fixed position.
3. While keeping your hands parallel, make a left-to-right sweeping motion with your hands. You are working from the wrists—your arms do not move.
4. (Finger Flow)
   a. Your hand is in an open position. Move to a closed hand position by moving the fingers one by one in a rhythmic motion. Begin with the little finger and end with a closed fist.
   b. Slowly open your hand in the same rhythmic motion and repeat.

10

POTPOURRI

This is the section where we have lumped together all the exercises that do not fit into any of the other categories. These exercises are enjoyable because they allow for a change in the otherwise normal routine.

From something as simple as treading water (for swimmers) to the all-purpose (all parts of the body) *Universal* with its varied routines, you should find something interesting in "Potpourri" to enhance your HYDROROBICS workout.

DEVICES

Hand paddles, ankle weights, weight belts, arm floats—any of these devices can be used to provide greater resistance in the water. If you are at A or B Fitness Level, you may wish to consider these devices for increasing your muscular strength and endurance capabilities.

INNER TUBE LAPS (Arms)

BODY PARTS	FITNESS LEVEL	FREQUENCY	SPEED
Arms, neck	A	*25 yds/8	moderate to fast
shoulders, back,	B	*25 yds/6	moderate
chest, stomach	C	*25 yds/4	slow

*average home pool size is approximately 20 yards long.

Starting Position (A)

Sit in an inner tube with your arms and legs extended over the tube.

Basic Exercise

1. Paddle yourself across the pool in laps according to your fitness level.
    a. For greater resistance, drag your feet in the water as you paddle.
    b. For greater muscle development in the stomach area, extend your legs out of the water at a slight incline.
2. Now paddle in the opposite direction.

Starting Position (B)

Turn over on to your stomach, lying flat across the inner tube. Your body should be straight and stiff with your feet out of the water.

Basic Exercise

1. Paddle yourself across the pool in laps:
    a. using the crawl stroke b. using the breast arm stroke
2. Alternate strokes, one lap at a time.

Starting Position (C)

Place the inner tube around your body near the waist or the breast area.

Basic Exercise

1. Lie on your stomach and paddle using the over arm crawl stroke.
2. Let your legs drag in the water for maximum resistance.
3. Turn over on your back and do a back crawl arm stroke.

INNER TUBE LAPS (Legs)

BODY PARTS	FITNESS LEVEL	FREQUENCY	SPEED
Hips, legs	A	25 yds/8	moderate to fast
	B	25 yds/6	moderate
	C	25 yds/4	slow

Starting Position

Place the inner tube around your body under your arms or under the breast area.

Basic Exercise

1. Lie on your stomach and kick across the pool using the flutter kick.
2. Turn over on your back and again use the flutter kick from this position.
3. Alternate with other kick strokes.

WATER TREADING
(for the swimmers)

BODY PARTS	FITNESS LEVEL	DURATION	SPEED
Major muscles in	A	5-10 minutes	n/a
the lower and	B	5 minutes	n/a
upper body	C	3-5 minutes	n/a

Basic Exercise

In deep water:
1. Tread water using both your arms and legs.
2. Tread water using only your legs.
3. Tread water using only your arms.

THE UNIVERSAL

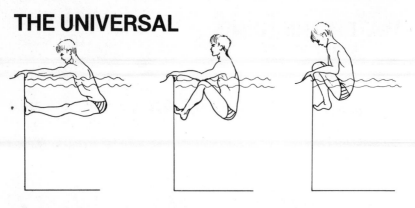

BODY PARTS	FITNESS LEVEL	FREQUENCY	SPEED
Entire body	A	10	Slow
	B	8	Slow
	C	6	Slow

Starting Position

Grasp the pool wall with both hands and place you feet flat on the wall about 12″ below your hands. Your legs are slightly bent in this position.

Basic Exercise

1. Try to straighten you legs and hold this position for approximately 8 seconds or longer but no more than 15 (static stretch). Be careful not to force your legs into this position.
2. Pull your body into a tuck position on the wall. Be sure your knees are between your arms. Yes, your heels are now off the wall.
3. Keep this position as you pull your body upward out of the water as far as possible. This will require a lot of arm and shoulder strength and may include some moaning and groaning. Hold this position for 8 seconds or more (isometric contraction). Congratulations, you've gotten this far. The rest is easier.
4. Drop down to the tuck position and back to the starting position.
5. Repeat 2,3,4 and 5, but eliminate the 8-second hold so that your body is in a continuous rhythmic 4-count motion (dynamic movements).

Variation

1. You can personalize this routine with double or triple   bobbing movements in #1 and #3.
2. While in starting position, swing your body in a left to right   motion. This will give added stretch to your legs and back.

PART THREE

HYDROROBICS
IS FOR
EVERYONE

11

WEIGHT CONSCIOUS: APPLYING THE MAGIC FORMULA

Some of you may want to lose weight. Some of you may want to gain. And of course some of you would like to maintain what you have—and still keep physically fit.

Essentially, we are all weight conscious, whether losing, gaining or maintaining. As you go through various stages of your life, you may discover that you have needed all three approaches to your weight. Certainly everyone hopes to reach the maintenance stage. You can—with the magic formula.

The catch is that the magic formula is both the same and different for everyone who uses it. It may even be the same and different for you as an individual in different stages of your life.

Alright, enough double-talk, you say. We confess we're leading you on because our formula is simple, the kind you have heard about before, and one you may not want to believe.

But it does work!

Since about half of the entire adult American population is *overweight*, let's deal with that problem first. We are not going to prescribe a special diet for you. If you have battled with excess weight, you already know that crash diets work for as long as it takes to go off the diet. You also know that more sensible diets can be boring enough to seem like they take forever to get results.

How about taking a serious look at what your eating habits really are before you go any further with this chapter.

What kind of foods do you really love to eat? What kind of foods do you eat the most of? How much junk food do you eat (compared to nutritious food)? What foods do you avoid? Why? How much *total* food do you eat? Has the amount gradually increased? Do you drink alcohol? More than you used to? Do you snack a lot? What kinds of snacks?

Sit down with a blank piece of paper and realistically create a summary of your eating habits. Think about the items that seem inconsequential in your diet but are adding unnecessary calories.

Is there something you eat habitually every day that you really don't need or want? Do you eat all the food that you've cooked, *even though you are full*, because you don't want to waste it? Yes, children are starving somewhere in the world, but you can't eat their share for them.

We think the concept of dieting for the rest of your life sounds like a miserable way to live. We both love to eat and to cook (in fact, we've discovered some great restaurants while writing this book!), and we think that you should enjoy those same pleasures if you want to.

So what do we do to keep the weight where it should be—to maintain? After all, no one will believe our claims as authors and instructors of a fitness concept if we don't look fit (for proof look at the front cover again).

Well, one of us is an athlete. Joe gets plenty of regular exercise teaching recreational sports, keeping up his fencing skills (a very strenuous sport that only looks easy), and enjoying many other recreational activities. That's fine for him, you say. He burns calories with all that activity. What about the rest of the world? Nonathletes are by far the majority of the population.

If you read the preface to this book you know that the other author is not an athlete. Not even a weekend athlete! As a matter of fact, Diane's lifestyle was totally devoid of any physical activity until she was introduced to HYDROROBICS. Now let's get down to serious considerations of diet.

Author Tells All

Diane was always the gym class misfit. She has a sedentary desk job and considers her main involvement in sports to be watching the Olympics on TV every four years. She has what her mother always called a "curvy" figure (Mother always was clever with words). When "curvy" started turning into "matronly," Diane discovered an easier way to control her weight. It has affected almost every aspect of her life.

Let's go back to the suggestion of analyzing your eating habits and use Diane as an example. She really thought she had a good dietary approach. She liked fruit and vegetables, she wasn't very excited about fried foods or junk food. She included foods from all of the food groups that every nutrition book or article recommends. But she did love desserts (and still does), and she did love to cook and bake (and still does), and the more she cooked and baked, the more she ate. Since she wasn't getting any exercise, she wasn't doing anything to keep those calories from turning curvy into matronly.

When her husband bought her a sweat suit and suggested she might like to join him in his regular running program, she knew she wasn't ready to become a matron.

Running was not for Diane so she tried HYDROROBICS. She knew she had found the exercise program she could stay with and enjoy. But "hydro" alone was not going to take off excess pounds. A change in eating habits had to come first!

Remember, she still cooks and bakes, and tries out new restaurants, and eats the foods she loves.

So what did she do? She alreay had a "balanced" diet. She just had too much of a good thing. She learned to serve herself smaller portions of food, to not clean up the last few spoonfuls in the pot, to share a luscious dessert with her dining partner, to use calories wisely.

Diane thinks french fries may be nice, but hot fudge sundaes are nicer. So she passes up the things she doesn't care about as much in order to eat the ones she does. She eats the foods she likes, but *she is not a dieter*. She is *weight conscious*.

She is eating for the pleasure food gives her and for the good health of a balanced diet. She is also aware of what part exercise plays in the formula that works for maintaining her weight.

HYDROROBICS is a three-times-a-week must for her formula. When work or travel or some other commitment prevents getting the third workout, she knows that some hot fudge may have to wait also.

"How much my balance of proper eating and regular exercise had become a necessity hit home when I took a 2-week vacation to a lovely part of New England without a swimming pool to be seen. I had to begin leading a post-vacation HYDROROBICS class with seven extra pounds to work off."

She has since discovered that you can find swimming pools almost everywhere. A little extra search can mean some very good vacation food and no regrets about the pool you left behind.

Let's get back to Joe, our athlete. Eating in restuarants with Diane and on his travels for the U.S. Olympic Committee sometimes means less time for his more vigorous exercise program. He, too, is weight conscious and knows that he must adjust his formula when he doesn't exercise in balance with his food intake.

At different times in their busy schedules, both the athlete and the nonathlete use the formula that works for each of them-eating the right amount of food and getting the right amount of exercise. It's the same and it's different.

The Scale Must Be Wrong!

Let's look at another example of finding the magic formula. You've already met *Barbara Gaston*, who was dieting and performing HYDROROBICS exercises with little early success at weight loss. Barbara was losing inches but not pounds.

It was hard for her to realize that the exercise she was doing was first tightening (toning) the muscles on her frame.

It just so happened that Barbara was gaining muscle mass equal to the amount of fat she was losing. *Physical Fitness, a Way of Life*, by Bud Getchell, explains that if she had been dieting without exercise, she would have been losing fat and lean body tissue, especially from muscles. And here's a bit of information you may not have known: *when you regain weight, it tends to be mostly fat*. So, without exercise, you lose both fat and muscle and regain just the fat. That's just one of the drawbacks of perpetual dieting.

Enough of the negative. How about some positive information about the combination of exercise and diet? According to the Health Maintenace Study conducted by Pacific Mutual Life Insurance Co., 80% of the dieters who are on a regular exercise program are successful with their diets. The study concludes that "an important benefit of regular exercise is that it makes it easier to diet successfully."

Exercise and Hunger

We must dispell the misconception about strenuous activity and resultant hunger. If you think exercise will increase your appetite and cause you to "blow the diet" you are wrong.

When you are exercising, you will not be any hungrier than you would have been without the exercise. And you are burning calories.

That information and some other good ideas about *Exercise and Weight Control* are available in a pamphlet put out by the President's Council on Physical Fitness and Sports, available from the U.S. Government Printing Office.

Water: Inside and Out

So much for increased appetite. You will, however, probably notice that you are thirstier than usual after exercising. Lucky you. Most of us don't drink enough water anyway.

What's so special about water, you may be thinking? After all, you drink coffee, soft drinks, orange juice for breakfast. Those are fluids. Right?

True, there is some water in all that. There is also a lot of something else—calories. And how about sugar? Caffeine?

Water has no calories, no sugar, no acid, and in most cases, is *very* inexpensive. When and why did drinking water go out of style? You will be less hungry after drinking a glass of water!

We know one woman who takes a coffee cup filled with water to her job-related meetings. Her co-workers thought it was strange, at first. They all drank coffee. They don't notice anymore. She knows it is one way to get some of her daily water intake.

Drinking enough water is another of those time-consuming habits that really can be incorporated into your routines, if you try putting them there. Try increasing your water intake for about a month, and see if you don't notice some changes, especially in your skin.

A handbook for coaches put out by the American Alliance for Health, Physical Education, Recreation and Dance called *Nutrition for Athletes* tells us that water is used in the digestive process, it carries nutrients to the tissues, carries waste out of the body and controls the body temperature. What happens without water? Your body will take water from itself—from the cells—and that quickly becomes dehydration. You've heard of dehydration?

You can certainly turn your new water habit into something classier than hanging around the kitchen faucet if you care about such things. Try ordering bottled water—perhaps with a slice of lemon or lime—the next time you're in a social situation. You haven't forgotten about the calories in alcohol, or have you?

Perfecting the Formula

Getting back to Barbara, who was firming up and losing inches without weight loss—don't be discouraged if you experience these same benefits. Weight loss should be gradual, and those firm muscles are more attractive (and healthier) than the thin, flabby tissue that often results from dieting without exercise.

You can expect to see gradual changes on a continuous basis, *if you continue* to practice your magic formula. Barbara saw immediate results. They just weren't the ones she had expected to see on her scale. It took some time for her to perfect the formula that was right for her.

So, what ingredients have we put into the formula so far?

- Exercise, naturally (that is what this book is about!).
- A balanced diet, or should we say "balanced eating habits."
- Water (the kind you drink, not the kind with chlorine in it).

What about vitamins? Dr. Sara Hunt, a nationally known nutritionist and a registered dietician at Georgia State University, tells her students that vitamins are okay as an insurance policy for making sure that the balanced diet has covered everything the body needs. But they really shouldn't be necessary if the proper food is consumed, and they should never be taken in "megadoses."

Besides, they're expensive. If you have extra money to spend on your nutritional needs, how about investing in fresh produce—or bottled water!

Dr. Hunt thinks the formula we're suggesting to you—exercise, balanced diet, lots of water—is a good one. She urges you to experiment with what works for you. And she cautions you to be careful if you've had terrible eating habits in the past.

Remember that Diane went back to "normal" eating on a smaller scale after achieving her ideal weight. But quantity was her only bad habit. If your old "normal" eating didn't include all the food groups and was heavy (we used that word on purpose) on potato chips and soft drinks, then you must re-program your eating style. It can still be fun. We've already told you we're not interested in perpetual dieting— just good, healthy (and delicious) eating to go along with the exercise in the formula. Try it.

What About the "Skinny" People?

If you think you are underweight, you are in the minority. You may need to gain weight for health reasons, and a physician would be the best guide for you on that decision.

But, if you have a naturally slim body and wish that you could add some inches in strategic locations, you also need to look at your eating habits and the kind of exercise you get.

Let us warn you though, as Sara Hunt points out, "It may be your genetic disposition to be slender." If you fall into that category, remember two things: (1) you are the envy of a lot of people, and (2) this does not necessarily mean "fit."

So, now that you've decided being thin isn't so bad after all, we've given you a new problem to worry about. As a thin person, you may have to work just as hard at becoming fit and maintaining fitness as the person with too many extra pounds.

You will have to develop your own magic formula with the same approach—analyzing your eating habits, planning ways to change or augment them, and involving regular exercise in your plan. You may especially want to emphasize the exercises that develop strength in certain parts of the body. Those exercises should develop or increase muscles to give you some extra weight.

But you're probably not as concerned with pounds as you are with appearance. This is where a gradual weight gain becomes just as important as a gradual weight loss.

Just as you may be genetically disposed to being thin, you may also be genetically disposed to losing and gaining weight in specific parts of your body first. You may want to put some weight on your legs and find that it has gone to your waist, or your face, or anywhere but the place you were hoping it would go.

That's why it is important for you to exercise every part of your body, even though you are placing special emphasis on certain target areas. A total fitness approach should result in a gain (or loss, or maintenance) of inches in proportion. It may even mean you will gain inches in some parts of your body and lose in others. And the total fitness approach of HYDROROBICS will also improve your cardiovascular fitness, strength and flexibility. We think you'll like the results.

Now, what about the ammunition your body will need to go along with the exercise? You will want to look carefully at adding fats, breads, cereals and other *healthy* foods for increasing calories. Those calories will be exercised into muscle instead of becoming fat, so you needn't worry about that.

Some eating tricks for weight gain that Sara Hunt shares with us include eating a snack closer to the last meal you ate rather than the meal you are going to eat. That's because you don't want to ruin your appetite for that next meal. A bedtime snack is another good way to add pounds. (Note: If you don't need to gain weight and you're reading this section, these are hints of what *not* to do!)

But remember, most of us probably have what Dr. Hunt calls the "set-point." It's the point toward which your body appears to move in weight—and then stops once that weight is reached. If you've reached your "set-point," and you are both healthy and physically fit, you are ready for the next stage of being weight conscious.

The Relaxation Benefit

There is a special benefit from exercising that seems to be especially important to the thin people.

If you are thin and have failed at attempts to gain weight, one factor may be tension. You may burn calories through anger, through internalizing and worrying about life's problems. We know one man who regularly has sleepless nights over world peace and other major problems he has no way to solve.

Exercise won't solve the problems, and we are not prepared to psychoanalyze you. *But*, many people include relaxation as a prime benefit of HYDROROBICS.

Diane Calhoun, who incorporates HYDROROBICS into her lunch hour whenever she can, says "I am a lot more relaxed in my life."

And Amy Iszagerri, who first started doing HYDROROBICS because of a hip problem that prevents running, remarked, "The water is so relaxing—I feel refreshed when I get out."

Some people find that it's important for them to get to the pool for "hydro" when they are most busy and have the least amount of time. Why? For the relaxation benefit. They are refreshed, renewed, relaxed and ready to take on whatever they have to deal with in a busy schedule.

The relaxation benefit doesn't assure you of extra pounds, but we've seen it work for some. Maybe it'll work for you.

Maintaining the Formula

Whether you have lost weight or gained, you will have to adjust your magic formula to maintain the new you.

This is the fun part! You will have the boost of knowing that you are healthier, fitter and looking terrific. People will tell you how good you look. In the last chapter, "How to Stay with It!" we will show you that this is one of the greatest rewards—one which will help motivate you to continue your exercise program.

You will have to experiment with how much and what kind of food will be a maintenance level for you. The given in the maintenance formula, however, is at least three times a week with your exercise program, the one you have designed for your fitness level. And don't rule out the possibility that your fitness level has changed. Unless you were at the "A" level to begin with, there is a good possibililty that you can do more now than when you first began your workouts.

HYDROROBICS is suitable for all fitness levels, probably one of the reasons you are attracted to it for your own fitness. As your body and ability changes, and as you continue to perform the exercises, you should be able to do more of the same or work more vigorously at the same, or do some exercises you thought you could never do.

As we told you, the magic formula is the same, but it's different. The important thing is that it works and it can work for you!

A Few Helpful Hints for Being "Weight Conscious"

- The way food is cooked is important (stir-fry is not only better for you than regular fried foods, it's quick and easy).
- What you put *on* foods can make a difference (the poor potato gets a lot of bad press from butter and sour cream).
- Do you really need all that salt!? (Experiment with herbs—and white wine for seasoning.)
- Fresh food versus processed food can make a caloric difference (fresh is great stir-fried!).
- Eat for you, not for the people around you who may be hungry at odd times and want company. (Mothers in particular have this problem.)
- Grocery shop from a list (buy only what's on the list) and only shop once each week (include a few "treats" and try to make them last *all* week).
- Remember our suggestion about using bottled water instead of alcohol (1 1/2 ounces of liquor = 150 calories *and* it stimulates the appetite).
- You don't have to be fanatical about cholesterol—if you are eating a balance of food types.
- Trust a full-length mirror more than a scale.

Some Ingredients for your Formula

Before you begin your weight gain/loss program, be sure to consult your physician.

At the end of this book, in the Appendix section, you will find some simple ingredients for applying the magic formula.

- How to calculate your ideal body weight
- How to calculate your caloric needs
- A sample 1200 calorie diet which includes all the basic food groups

Remember, these are just suggested helpers. *You* will determine if the ideal weight on the scale is really right for *you*, and *you* will be weight conscious enough to adapt *your* eating habits to the formula that works for *you*.

If you need some extra help at this point, read the chapter entitled "How to Stay With It!" And if it works, write to us and tell us *your* story.

References

American Alliance for Health, Physical Education, Recreation and Dance. *Nutrition for Athletes*. Washington, D.C.: AAHPERD 1971.
Louis Harris and Associates, Inc. *Health Maintenance Study*. Pacific Mutual Life Insurance Co., 1978.
President's Council on Physical Fitness and Sports. *Exercise and Weight Control*. Washington, D.C.: U. S. Government Printing Office, 1976.

Consultant

Sara M. Hunt, Ph.D.
Nutritionist & Registered Dietician
Georgia State University

PREGNANCY: BEFORE, DURING AND AFTER

Remember Diane Day from Chapter 2? She began her HYDRORO-BICS program during the 7th month of her pregnancy. In this section, we'd like to look at the benefits of "hydro" if you are pregnant, planning a pregnancy, or trying to exercise your postpartum body into its prepregnancy condition.

If you're at any stage of the "having a baby" part of your life, this is a good time to begin a regular HYDROROBICS workout program and to keep it a part of your total conditioning plan. There are several reasons why exercising in the water is particularly suited to pregnancy and has been the time when many women first discovered HYDROROBICS. Others were already using "hydro" when they became pregnant. Let's look at this latter group first.

Getting Ready for Pregnancy—or Planned Parenthood Takes to the Water

All the reasons we have given for exercising, especially for exercising with HYDROROBICS, are also good for the woman who is planning a pregnancy. If you are in good cardiorespiratory condition, have increased the strength and flexibility of your muscles, and have attained your ideal weight, your baby is going to begin life with the best chance for health. That should be obvious.

We are concerned with not only the baby, but the effects of pregnancy on you. If you begin your pregnancy in good physical condition, you will find that getting back to that condition after the birth will take less time and will be easier to do.

So many women plan their pregnancies to fit into careers, educational goals and the most appropriate stages of their marriages—there is plenty of opportunity to add consideration of your body's condition, your overall physical fitness, into that planning.

One very obvious concern in planning a pregnancy is to minimize the possibility of infertility. You may have read about the effects of running on some women's menstrual cycles. If irregular cycles and a lessened chance for pregnancy are results of exercise, many women will be seriously discouraged from opting for fitness at critical times in their lives.

You don't have to stop exercising if you want to become pregnant! We were assured by Dr. Edwin Dale, Associate Professor of Gynecology-Obstetrics, School of Medicine, Emory University, that this problem has been related primarily to running and strenuous dance. He also assured us that the probable cause for irregular cycles—excessive heat—is eliminated in the cooler temperatures of water. So, read on.

Although HYDROROBICS is a total fitness program, to prepare for pregnancy you may want to put special emphasis on the middle body exercises. If you've had problems with back pain, your doctor will advise you on what to avoid. Otherwise, strengthening the lower back muscles will provide needed support and less discomfort during the pregnancy. You may want to include the *Figurehead* and the *Universal* in your program. Read the "Body Parts" at the top of each exercise to find more ways to work the lower back.

The abdominal muscles are an obvious area to be strengthened prior to pregnancy. They are also one of the body parts most people need to exercise at any stage of life. Improper posture, sitting down all day at a desk, a few extra pounds, lack of exercise—all contribute to the famous "pot belly" syndrome. But stronger abdominal muscles before pregnancy will be better prepared to support the growing weight of the baby during pregnancy, and will more readily return to their normal condition after the birth. The uterus will gradually return to its prepregnancy size without exercise, but the muscles supporting the uterus will need some help from you. If you are used to exercise and the muscles have been toned before stretching of the abdomen, they can easily be exercised back into condition.

Some of the special mid-body exercises that strengthen the abdomen include *Six Count Twister* and *Double Leg Lift*.

The Whole Nine Months!!

We've mentioned before—you can and should exercise during the nine months of pregnancy (unless your physician advises against it because of conditions for your specific pregnancy).

A study discussed in *Exercise During Pregnancy: Effects on the Fetus* by Edwin Dale, Karen M. Mullinax and David H. Bryan, all with Emory University in Atlanta, Georgia, revealed that "there were no significant differences between runners and nonrunners with respect to weight gain during pregnancy, length of labor and delivery and incidence of obstetric complication." Exercise of some type is safe and usually recommended for pregnant women.

As soon as your pregnancy is confirmed, you'll want to inform your doctor that you are exercising. You will most likely receive a go-ahead to continue your fitness program. If that program is HYDROROBICS, your go-ahead should continue for the full term.

If you have not been involved in HYDROROBICS before your pregnancy, there are many excellent reasons to begin a program of water exercise now.

One reason to select HYDROROBICS as your pregnancy exercise program is that you can safely begin it at a time when you really shouldn't begin a vigorous exercise program at all. Our favorite obstetrician, Z. B. Newton, normally recommends that his patients continue whatever vigorous exercise they have been doing, but "not begin anything new during pregnancy." But you won't have the same dangers in water that you would have in traditional land exercises. You can begin HYDROROBICS at any point in the pregnancy, using common sense and your own physician's advice.

You will *feel* safe exercising in the water. This is important. You will also feel buoyant and have ease of movement. This is especially important during the latter months of your pregnancy when you may not feel as light on your feet as you would like.

One of the most important reasons for selecting "hydro" during pregnancy is that you will be able to continue it through the entire nine months. It is a total form of exercise, dealing with all parts of the body and all aspects of fitness, yet can be accomplished without danger of injury. Of course, there are reasons to be considered by nonpregnant women as well, but they are especially important during your pregnancy.

All the reasons why you will feel good doing HYDROROBICS, at any time, apply now. But they will become especially important during pregnancy. You will be feeling good; you will be keeping your muscles toned and strong; you will be keeping your weight under control; and you will be doing all this safely and comfortably.

An extra bonus: In warm weather, spending time in the water will be refreshing.

Speaking of warmth, be aware of the temperature of the water. Edwin Dale urges you to avoid hot water, especially in the early months of pregnancy when a growing embryo can be damaged by excessive heat. The water should feel cool when you begin to exercise. If it feels like bath water, it's probably too warm, and hot tubs are definitely out if you are pregnant.

Whereas your specific condition requires that you suspend other physical activities, you will probably be **able** to continue "hydro" with little variation in your routine. One example of using "hydro" as the constant in her physical fitness program during pregnancy is shared by Libby Billingsley, who began a HYDROROBICS program during the 6th month of her third pregnancy. She had taken a "hydro" course during her first pregnancy, but chose aerobics and biking during the months before the birth of her second child. Libby continued with these activities between pregnancies but again went back to "hydro" for the third pregnancy. By the 7th month of this third pregnancy, her physician had recommended that she discontinue the biking and make some adjustment to the kinds of water exercises she performed, especially the exercises that caused stress to her lower back.

For Libby, the advantages of HYDROROBICS during pregnancy included feeling better, being less tired and exercising "comfortably." As an added bonus, it turned out to be the one exercise she could continue longer than the others. Libby was in a HYDROROBICS class on a Tuesday, and gave birth to a healthy baby girl on Wednesday.

You will most likely find the variety of water exercises available to you in the HYDROROBICS program a definite advantage during pregnancy. You will have to add creativity to your fitness plan by varying the exercises you include according to the stage of pregnancy and your obstetrician's advice.

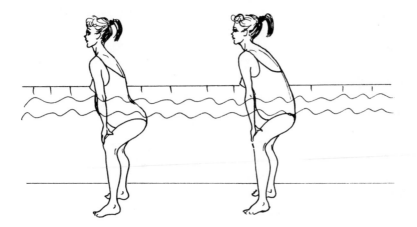

Both Diane Day and Libby Billingsley found that *The Universal*, so comfortable to do during the early and middle stages of pregnancy, became somewhat awkward as their bodies changed in shape. It is almost impossible to pull the body to the pool wall with the knees tucked to the chest when a very large abdomen is in the way. But they were able to continue with the first position, the leg stretch portion of that exercise.

Libby's physician also warned her to avoid certain exercises midway through her 7th month. She was already being cautious about anything that put unnecessary strain on her lower back. But she was vigorously jogging (*Joggernaut*) and performing the rest of the aerobic exercises long after she had to give up her land activities. Zack Newton tells us that you might be able to continue exercising with practically no program changes throughout the pregnancy. Remember what everyone tells you when you're pregnant, "Every pregnancy is different."

A Word About Aerobics

You can continue aerobics during pregnancy. It is through aerobics that you work the cardiorespiratory component of your physical fitness. You continue to maximize the efficiency of your heart and lungs and, as a result, the capacity of your body to deal with exercise. Water allows you to continue maintaining this aspect of fitness without danger, even if you find that the other exercises have become awkward or uncomfortable. Achieving your training pulse rate during aerobics is not harmful. If, however, your pulse rate remains high after you stop exercising, contact your doctor right away. The emphasis you place on strong regular breathing in aerobic exercises is going to help you during labor when breathing properly can lessen pain and ease the birth process. Remember, you are in control of the force and effort that you put into any of the HYDROROBICS exercises. This may be the time to gradually slow down the pace and the force, without eliminating an activity.

If you are already well along in your pregnancy and struggling with an assortment of aches and pains, you might find what Barbara Jean Cooper-Newton told us interesting. Barbara Jean is an OGN Nurse Practitioner who frequently counsels the patients in her husband's OB-GYN practice. "When they call about ligament pain or muscle pain, I always ask if they are exercising," she explained, "and I can almost guess what the answer will be."

The women most likely to have discomforts during pregnancy are the ones who are not in good shape to begin with and who are not doing anything positive to avoid those physical discomforts. Strong muscles will adapt to changes caused by pregnancy more readily and with fewer aches and pains. You will find that a gentle form of exercise can make a difference in your pregnancy, even if you've never exercised before. And, of course, if you have been exercising, you'll really benefit from more of the same—for the whole nine months.

When to Stop?

We've already touched on when to stop exercising with HYDRORO-BICS, but we'll say it again. You can continue your exercise program in the water until you go into labor. Once the membranes rupture or leak, you will be risking infection. Until then, you are relatively safe in the protective atmosphere of the water. Don't forget to ask your doctor about what is right for you.

When to Start Again?

As soon as possible. If you have a private pool, you may want to begin immediately. If you are using a public pool, you'll probably wait a couple of weeks. If you have not had an episiotomy, you can begin exercising as soon as you feel ready. Again, check with your physician.

Do we have to tell you the reasons why so many women choose "hydro" as their postpregnancy exercise? The first is that they can quickly return to exercise and to the shape that has gotten a little "out of shape."

Exercising in the water is particularly suited to pregnancy.

You could probably think of many more reasons to select "hydro" after pregnancy. Most of them are the same reasons why everyone would choose it. For Catherine Andreen, it took ten months after the birth of her daughter to decide on any serious exercise program.

"I had reached my prepregnancy weight within two months after the birth, but I still felt flabby and out of shape." Catherine has been an active participant in a HYDROROBICS class at the university where she works for some time now. "I was sure 'hydro' worked when I stopped doing it for a few weeks. I noticed a definite deterioration in the strength of my stomach muscles."

Although she found HYDROROBICS in the postpregnancy stage of her life, Catherine plans to include it in all stages of pregnancy. "If I have another pregnancy," she assures us, "I would like to try to continue with 'hydro' during the pregnancy."

We think you will enjoy making HYDROROBICS a special and very important part of the "having a baby" part of your life too.

References

Dale, E.; Mullinax, K. M.; and Bryan, D. H. *Exercise During Pregnancy: Effects on the Fetus*. Atlanta: Emory University School of Medicine, 1982.

Department of Physical Therapy. *Preparing for Delivery*. Atlanta: Georgia Baptist Medical Center, 1981.

Noble, Elizabeth. *Essential Exercises for the Childbearing Year*. Boston: Houghton Mifflin Co., 1976.

Shanghold, Mona M. "Pregnancy." In *Sports Medicine for the Athletic Female*. Edited by Christine E. Haycock. Oradell, N.J.: Medical Economics Co., 1980.

Consultants

Alice Bowen
Senior Physical Therapist, RPT, M.Ed.
Department of Physical Medicine & Rehabilitation
Georgia Baptist Medical Center

Barbara Jean Cooper-Newton
OGN Nurse Practitioner

Edwin Dale, PhD.
Department of Gynecology & Obstetrics
Emory University School of Medicine

Z. B. Newton III, M.D.
Chairman, Department of Obstetrics & Gynecology
Georgia Baptist Medical Center

HEALTH PROBLEMS: A PANACEA?

If you've always been healthy, you may be wondering why we would include a chapter about various medical conditions in a book about physical fitness. The answer is simple. Not only is it possible to be healthy without being physically fit, it is also possible to be physically fit without being completely healthy.

You may have a specific medical condition that means you are not in perfect health. But for many conditions, that problem does not exclude you from seeking and achieving fitness.

We've included brief sections on a few of these conditions because we've found that many of our HYDROROBICS students have had these medical problems. For some it meant that they were finally discovering a form of exercise that would not aggravate their medical condition. For others it even meant a lessening of some of their symptoms.

Not Hydrotherapy

Again, we must stress that HYDROROBICS is not hydrotherapy. Before you begin an exercise program of any type, check with your physician about any special limitations you may have.

We think you'll find that the adaptability and safety of "hydro" will suit the needs of most people who are able to exercise. Nonswimmers as well as swimmers can take advantage of the water as a means of exercise.

Although HYDROROBICS is not hydrotherapy, it is important to understand both the differences and the connections between the two uses of water.

The exact origin of hydrotherapy is not known, but one text, Exercise in Water, edited by M. H. Duffield, discusses how Hippocrates (460-375 B.C.) used hot and cold water to treat diseases. Numerous sources refer to water therapy from the Graeco-Roman era to the baths and spas of the more modern Europeans.

Currently, hydrotherapy is used in supervised medical settings throughout the world to treat a large variety of illnesses and medical disorders. The therapy may be as simple as walking in water or as involved as prescribed movements.

We don't know exactly when the first water exercise, just for the sake of exercise, was performed. We suspect it evolved partly from the need for a more therapeutic form of exercise and partly from the joyful experience of playing in water.

Our approach with HYDROROBICS is one of exercise in a safe medium. We also think it is indeed a joyful experience. Perhaps both these elements will combine to give you the program you need for a safe route to physical fitness.

Remember, we are only mentioning here the health problems that are usually not aggravated by exercise in the water. If you have a medical condition that is not included in this chapter, consult your physician about exercise for you.

Orthopedic Problems

You may be one of many Americans with an orthopedic impairment that prevents you from enjoying an ordinary lifestyle. Your problem might result from a congenital malformation or from a serious accidental injury that has left you with some permanent musculoskeletal damage. Perhaps you have the type of orthopedic problem that can be corrected with time. In this case, normal or near-normal function may eventually be restored. In order to help you gain this normal function, your physician has most likely suggested or prescribed some form of exercise. Assuming that you will be allowed to exercise in an unsupervised setting, your big decision will be to choose a type of exercise.

Orthopedic problems may temporarily or permanently cause loss of some mobility in some part of your body. Since exercise involves a great deal of movement, people with a problem may tend to shy away from physical activity because it becomes too awkward—and may even cause pain. You may very well understand this because it has happened to you. Perhaps you even tried some type of traditional exercise activity or recreational sport and found it just didn't work for you.

Well, we can't promise you anything, but if you're willing to try HYDROROBICS, you might just find a pleasant surprise. Let's consider Barbara Jean Cooper-Newton's experience with HYDRORO-BICS.

Barbara Jean, a nurse and mother of three children, developed a serious back problem which severely affected her daily activity, especially her regular running exercise program. After living with severe bouts of pain for the first three weeks, she finally decided to seek medical advice. Her physician diagnosed her problem as involving the 4th and 5th lumbar vertebrae and disc pressure on the sciatic nerve. Knowing this, she decided to consult a physical therapist, who recommended that she start exercising by walking in chest deep water.

After a few sessions in the water, Barbara Jean began to experience immediate improvement of her condition. She found she could move more easily in the water, without the unnecessary pressure on the spinal nerves. This meant reduced pain.

For eight months Barbara Jean exercised in her home pool until she was finally able to swim laps. She began to gain more and more function from her lower back, allowing her to enjoy more of her normal daily activities. Then Barbara Jean discovered HYDRORO-BICS. With her physical therapist's approval, she added a modified "hydro" program to her regular exercise routine.

Although it took Barbara Jean two years, she finally reached the point of being her "old self." She has gone back to running occasionally. Now she has a new goal—to lose most of the extra weight she gained from not being able to exercise aerobically in her first year of disability. How? Barbara Jean says, "By continuing to do a balanced program of running and HYDROROBICS!" Like Barbara Jean Cooper-Newton, several students who have taken HYDROROBICS at Georgia State University over the years began with similar types of orthopedic problems. The majority of these people lived with their problem for years and tried other forms of exercise only to find their problem easily aggravated. This usally prevented them from developing their physical fitness.

When these people try HYDROROBICS, they're impressed with how they can improve their cardiorespiratory system—and even feel good after a workout.

They enjoy not having the muscle soreness and pain generally associated with exercise. What's more, they find that their orthopedic problem doesn't limit their movement as much in water as in other forms of exercise.

As you will learn when you read "Injury—You Don't Have to Give up Exercise," the physical properties of water help explain why exercising in water is so beneficial for people with medical problems. For example, the buoyant force of water helps you move easily. This means you can control the amount of stress applied to your body much more easily in the water environment. This allows you to compensate for your medical problem. With minor adjustments, you can usually continue to exercise with the intensity necessary to develop your cardiorespiratory fitness — even your total fitness!

So, if you have some type of orthopedic problem, why not read on and consider the many other benefits of HYDROROBICS. Especially read the chapter on "Designing Your Personalized Program" to help you get started. Remember, if your medical problem gets worse when you exercise, check with your doctor.

Exercising and Heart Problems

Tony, a school teacher and regular physical fitness buff, developed a heart problem called arrhythmia; he was going through some diffi-cult times in his life. He was always very healthy and in excellent physical condition—or at least he thought so. His arrhythmia, or irregular heart beat, was diagnosed as being stress induced and occurred frequently during the first few months after the onset. For the first time in Tony's life, he began to realize the impact stress can have on your body.

Tony reluctantly modified his daily routine because of his heart condition. At first, he felt so drained of energy that it took all he could do just to keep up with his job. Almost all his physical fitness activities were severely curtailed because too often they would trigger his arrhythmia. Once this happened he had to immediately stop play and take his medication. Tony found this extremely frustrating. He kept saying, "How could this happen to me? I'm young and in excellent physical shape."

After a few months, Tony adjusted somewhat to his external stress factors and could slowly resume exercising. He had often read that exercise seemed to be a catharsis for many people, helping to reduce their anxiety-tension levels. So exercise, along with some mind control techniques, was how Tony elected to combat his prob-lem.

For several months Tony continued to play racquetball, tennis, and to run, but he found his arrhythmia problem still there. It was like Russian Roulette; he never knew when his heart would "kick off" into the irregular heartbeat. Tony began to think that maybe the types of activities he was choosing were too physically demanding or too competitive. So he discussed the situation with his cardiologist. It was agreed that Tony should try some other form of exercise, like swimming. Swimming, he was told, is less competitive and enables you to escape from the real world and its pressures. Then, too, the rhythmic motion of the water over the body tends to help you relax.

That was good enough for Tony. He started to swim the next day. In addition to swimming, Tony joined a HYDROROBICS class he saw in session each time he visited the pool. He did it as a change of pace and was pleasantly surprised at the results. It's been over a year now, and fortunately, Tony has only had one or two incidences of arrhythmia. Exercise seems to be working for Tony.

Tony is only one of millions of Americans who experience a heart problem each year. Their conditions range from mild to severe. Maybe it's partly due to the fast-paced American way of living, because we tend to try to be #1 at everything we do. It's unfortunate that Americans have distinguished themselves with the unwanted statistic of being the country with the third highest heart mortality rate in the world. Over 1,000,000 heart attacks are counted each year, resulting in approximately 640,000 deaths. This makes coronary heart disease the leading cause of death in the United States.

Since there are over 20 varieties of heart disease, such as coronary heart disease and hypertensive heart disease, it would be impossible to discuss them in detail in this section. What's more important, there is much more to be learned about the causes and cures for heart attacks. It's well known that our living habits involve a certain number of factors associated with the incidence of heart attacks. These factors are commonly referred to as risk factors. The strongest risk factors are smoking, high blood pressure, stress, lack of exercise, and an excess of cholesterol and fatty acids in the blood. A person who has a combination of two or more risk factors is considered to be investing in a short lifespan. How many of the risk factors do you have?

If one of your risk factors is physical inactivity, chances are you may be courting the other risk factors without knowing it. It is a basic belief among exercise experts that exercise can help to control blood pressure, obesity, and the levels of fat substances in the blood—e.g., cholesterol, triglycerides, and high density lipoproteins (HDL'S)—often associated with heart disease. If this is true, then you should strongly consider adding exercise to your weekly schedule.

For more information on the value of exercise, read the first chapter in this book entitled, "Exercise: What's in it for Me?"

Well, if you have some type of cardiac problem and now realize the importance of exercise, it's time to get started. We are pleased that you are considering HYDROROBICS, but would like to call your attention to some concerns before you jump into the pool.

Supervised Versus Unsupervised Exercise

Exercise will be beneficial to you whether your heart problem is mild or serious. However, if your problem is serious, you should pursue an exercise program in a specialized cardiac rehabilitation facility. You will need to have special heart monitoring equipment available to determine your heart's response during activity. Under the supervision of a cardiologist, you'll be given the best medical attention, particularly if an emergency occurs.

If you have a mild heart problem and your doctor's approval to exercise, you may begin to do so in an unsupervised setting. This will put greater responsibility on you to make sure that you pursue your exercise program with caution. Don't overdo exercise at first. Take it slow and build up gradually. Remember, exercise begins as soon as you enter the water. The water's pressure will begin to overload your cardiorespiratory system, increasing your respiration and circulation.

Medication

If you take medication for your heart problem, e.g., digoxin or beta blockers, be aware that this medication will affect your training pulse rate. High blood pressure medication, for example, tends to lower your pulse rate during exercise. This low reading could lead you astray, causing you to reach dangerously high levels of physiological stress during exercise.

If you are on medication and wish to exercise, ask your doctor about having an EKG (electrocardiogram) stress test. This test will help your physician recommend a safe training pulse rate while you are on medication.

Identifying Heart Symptoms During Exercise

We wouldn't have included any information on this topic if it were not for a local Atlanta cardiologist who directed us to research on some cardiac patients who had difficulty in detecting ischemic heart symptoms during swimming. The research article, "The Effect of Swimming on Patients with Ischemic Heart Disease" originated in Stockholm, Sweden. One of the major conclusions stated that, "The subjective comfort and large muscle groups involved make swimming a good exercise, but the high relative energy cost and failure to identify ischemic symptoms indicate caution in cardiac patients, especially if their swimming skills are poor."

Although the research was conducted on swimming, we feel there might be similar implications for you when you perform HYDRORO-BICS. It appears that the activity of water passing over your chest and/or the rhythmic movements of the arms may act as a counterirritant, decreasing the chance of detecting ischemic symptoms. Until specific research is available on HYDROROBICS, we recommend that you give extra attention to this matter when exercising.

Routine Checkup

It will be important for you to stay in touch with your cardiologist as you progress in your "hydro" program. Call your cardiologist whenever some strange symptom occurs and get an opinion on the matter. As you improve your physical fitness, discuss with your physician to what degree you should increase your exercise intensity. See what we mean by routine checkups?!

Your physician will probably want to schedule you for a periodic physical to determine the effects your exercise is having on you. If you've been exercising consistently, we bet you'll look forward to this meeting, just to hear your doctor praise you on the wonderful gains you've made.

Stress as a Health Factor

There is little doubt that excessive stress is a factor in your health. Actually, many of the health conditions discussed in this chapter are aggravated by stress. That's why we want you to be aware of it.

The pressures, tensions, deadlines, and demands of daily living may be something you can not realistically eliminate from your life, and a certain amount is probably necessary to keep your life exciting.

But, you can deal with these stress factors in positive ways to minimize their effect on you and your health.

Dr. Phillip Wierson, director of the Counseling Center at Georgia State University, tells us that, "Anxiety can be a motivator, and can also be viewed as a signal that change needs to occur, that we need to take action for our own good. The task is to manage anxiety more effectively. We increasingly refer clients in therapy to exercise programs and recreational pursuits for reducing tension levels."

A good way to relax and reduce tension is through physical exercise. According to Frank Vitale's *Individualized Fitness Programs*, vigorous exercise can lessen the detrimental effects of stress in several ways. One way is, of course, by strengthening the body and preparing it to fight off stress. The other obvious way exercise works on stress is by "working it off." What does that mean? Well, when we asked people who performed HYDROROBICS for their opinion about "hydro," the majority of them mentioned feeling relaxed as one of the benefits. This was important to them. It should be important to you too.

As you establish a regular HYDROROBICS program you will probably notice a difference in how you feel in general. Part of that feeling will be relaxation. A woman we know, Pat Sartain, uses "hydro" for relaxation and that good feeling. As the director of an active university alumni association, she finds her busiest and most stressful time of the year to be the annual alumni fund drive. This is the time Pat says she needs to exercise the most—when she is busiest. She first began exercising for physical fitness, but has stayed with HYDROROBICS because, "It makes me feel good."

Pat Sartain and others like her are recognizing that physical activity can reduce the effects of stressful lives. We think stress belongs in this chapter on health as a reminder to you that it can create health problems—and that it doesn't have to.

Several case studies, recorded by Ira H. Wilson and Fred W. Kasch of San Diego State University, show the positive effects of water on a number of medical conditions, including severe stress. We're not claiming that HYDROROBICS or any other form of physical exercise is the only way to reduce stress. Many people turn to such methods of stress reduction as medication, mental imagery, self-hypnosis, yoga, personal counseling and finding new ways to communicate with those close to them. For some, relieving stress may be as simple and pleasurable as going to the kitchen and stirring up a batch of cookies.

Obviously, "hydro" is less fattening than the cookies method. We also think that a method of stress reduction and relaxation that has the extra bonus of improving your physical condition stands above the others. The more physically fit you are, the more prepared your body is to deal with the physiological side effects that accompany the stressful conditions in your life. We also think that the massage effect as your body moves through the water adds an extra stress reducer to your "hydro" plan.

You may want to combine more than one method of relaxing and reducing the tensions of stress. If you insist on baking (and eating) those cookies, you can work off the calories with HYDROROBICS.

But our main objective in this chapter is not weight control. Be sure you don't let stress aggravate a current medical condition or activate a new one. Be aware of stress as a factor in your good health.

Arthritis and HYDROROBICS

In an interview with officials from the Atlanta-based Arthritis Foundation, we learned that there are over 100 different types of arthritic conditions. If you have arthritis, and many of us do, this becomes significant for your choice of exercise. You have to be extremely careful with the form of exercise and the exercise environment you select, since what is good for one type of arthritis might be harmful to another type.

Arthritis may be generally defined as the inflammation of a joint. The degree of inflammation can range from a localized to a general condition. Regardless of your specific condition, you will most likely be encouraged to exercise. A pamphlet written by the Arthritis Foundation entitled, *Arthritis—the Basic Facts*, points out that a person who has arthritis must find the perfect balance between exercise and rest. If you're planning on doing a HYDROROBICS exercise program because of its therapeutic qualities, consult your physician and health professional. When you show your doctor the variety of exercises in this book, ask for advice on properly selecting a workout plan for your particular needs and limitations.

For example, Gladys Nuggles, a woman in her mid-fifties, decided to emphasize the finger and wrist exercises in the Upper Body section to deal with the problem of arthritic finger joints. After ten weeks of HYDROROBICS, Gladys found that her hands had, "more flexibility and less pain and stiffness. I can squeeze my fingers all the way down to my palm."

One bit of advice your physician will probably give you is to be particularly concerned with the temperature of the water. Your specific arthritic condition can be adversely affected if the water temperature is too warm or too cold. Your physician can suggest the best temperature for your situation. As a general water temperature guideline for athritic conditions, we consulted a specialized water exercise program manual entitled, *Twinges in the Hinges*, developed by the Southern California Chapter of the Arthritis Foundation. The manual suggests that the water temperature should be a minimum of 84 degrees, with a preferred temperature range of 86-88 degrees. The air temperature in a pool environment should be between 78-82 degrees, and without any drafts.

Remember, you shouldn't be too "gung-ho" to start your program. You'll have to go slowly at first and only later increase your intensity. When your arthritic condition "flares up," you'll want more rest and less exercise. The main advantage of "hydro" for you is that you'll probably be able to continue exercising *mildly*, even when your joints are bothering you. It will be important to move your limbs through the full range of motion whenever possible. "Hydro" will let you easily control the speed of movement and resistance in the water. The water's buoyancy will make it easier to move your outstretched limbs.

Always acknowledge the *pain response* when exercising. Listen to your body. If exercising is too painful, either limit it or stop exercising until your condition improves. It would be wise to consult your physician for suggestions on ways to avoid the cause of pain during exercise.

Most people with arthritic or similar health problems find HYDROROBICS a pleasing and rewarding form of exercise. Remember, you may have difficult moments when exercising, but if you can muster up the determination and patience to continue, you will experience a more healthful and invigorating life. Many students of HYDROROBICS who have suffered from arthritis have discovered much relief from their painful conditions. We will always remember Jean Johnson, who told us she couldn't even bend down to pick up an object from the floor because of her severe arthritis. After six weeks of HYDROROBICS, she came to us after class with a huge smile on her face and said, "Last evening was the first time in a long time that I was able to bend and pick up a towel I dropped on the floor."

We hope you can find the same success!

Lower Back Problems

This health problem should probably be included in the orthopedic section, but because of its preponderance, we decided to address it as a special topic.

There isn't much we can tell you about this health problem, except that 80% of low back problems are muscular in nature. The usual medical diagnosis is that weak abdominal muscles allow the pelvis to tilt forward, causing an extreme arch in the lower back. This arch puts the spinal cord out of proper alignment, resulting in undue stress on the spinal nerves—and that means *pain*.

Most low back problems can be corrected by strengthening your abdominal muscles and practicing good posture. HYDROROBICS can help you to do this, but discuss your approach with your physician or orthopedist. You'll want to be sure to avoid the HYDRORO-BICS exercises that can place a strain on the lower back. Otherwise, follow your exercise program routinely and notice the difference in just a few weeks.

Severe Obesity

Yes, we consider severe obesity to be a medical problem.

If you have an extreme weight problem, you are probably on the verge of a number of other medical problems as well. Or maybe your physician has already given you the news about a few conditions that you thought were caused by bad luck or divine intervention, but were really a direct result of that excess weight. We are not going to lecture you about your weight, though we do urge you to read the chapter on being weight conscious. It is quite possible that your weight is a result of glandular or other health problem causes. If so, you and your physician have probably established the limitations of your condition.

For you, exercise in the water may be the only possible way to vigorously move. The buoyant forces of water will help support your body. And you'll probably enjoy the feeling of being lighter in the water—as much as 90% lighter!

Specifically, the ease of movement in water means you will feel less stress to your joints when you are jumping and exercising aerobically. And all of the exercises will be easier to do in water compared to on land, where you are fighting gravity instead of being supported by the water's buoyancy.

You will certainly appreciate the bonus enjoyed by everyone who does HYDROROBICS, less discomfort and soreness of muscles.

What we hope you will find in the water is a new way to feel good about yourself and to begin to improve your overall physical fitness. Be sure to ask your doctor about any exercise limitations for your condition. You'll probably get a lot of encouragement to try HY-DROROBICS.

HYDROROBICS and Multiple Sclerosis

"Don't get over-tired! And of course don't get overheated! But be sure to exercise, or your limbs will get stiff!"

If you have Multiple Sclerosis (MS from here on), you've heard those warnings in some form or other. So how do you put all that advice to work? How do you exercise without overheating? Just the thought of exercise makes you feel tired, especially on those days when the word "fatigue" has a very special meaning for you.

Multiple Sclerosis is a disease of the central nervous system which normally occurs in young adults. It is erratic in its severity, but symptoms may include numbness, weakness of limbs, fatigue, vision problems and possible effects to almost every part of the body. Many people with MS lead normal lives without obvious evidence of a medical problem.

You must, by now, realize that we think HYDROROBICS is probably the perfect exercise program for you, the person with MS. But our enthusiasm is supported by many others—therapists, physicians, patients—who are more interested in the problems of MS than in the promotion of water exercise.

Let's begin with a statement from *RX-Therapeutic Claims in Multiple Sclerosis*, the most recent and authoritative document on MS, published by the International Federation of Multiple Sclerosis Societies (IFMSS) in 1982. It reads, "Aquatic therapy is nearly ideal because of temperature control, wide range of muscle groups involved, and diminished fatigue factor."

Sounds good. But it also sounds like they're talking about "therapy," not exercise. You are probably one of the many MS patients with the benign form of MS which allows you a nearly normal lifestyle. Or perhaps you're in a remission period and have no MS symptoms at all. You don't want therapy! You want to stay healthy and physically fit without bringing on the symptoms of the disease.

We talked with someone who knows about both—therapy and exercise—Dr. Sam Wright, a physician whose medical specialty is rehabilitation medicine at Emory University's Rehabilitation Center in Atlanta, Georgia. He says, "I'm a water proponent," and calls water exercise "one of the best forms of general exercise you can get." More from Dr. Wright later.

How about a patient's opinion? One of the most read MS patients is the Pulitzer Prize winning author, the late Miriam Ottenberg, whose *The Pursuit of Hope* has been almost like a bible to so many persons diagnosed as having MS. For Miriam and many of the people she talked with as she researched her book, there were two forms of exercise that seemed best suited to the needs of someone with MS. One was Yoga, with its emphasis on stretching, flexibility, and relaxation. The other was activity in the water. Why? Let's look at water and all the good things we've talked about, but as they pertain to the problems of MS.

Why Water?

We've already touched on temperature, use of muscles and less risk of fatigue. An understanding of the how's and why's of their importance will help you make the best use of your energy and your efforts at staying physically fit.

First, of course, you must already understand that a person with MS can be physically fit in every other way. If you didn't think that, you most likely would not have bothered to pick up a book on physical fitness. And, regular exercise is a very necessary factor in achieving and maintaining that physical fitness.

As we review the components of physical fitness (cardiorespiratory endurance, flexibility, muscular strength and endurance) discussed in other chapters, you should be pleased to know that every one of them is possible for you, even when you have MS symptoms. As Miriam Ottenberg points out in her section on exercise, "The disease affects nerve fibers rather than the muscles." It is, in fact, important to use those muscles and to strengthen them wherever possible. There will be times when you feel weak. But that is not because you are not strong. A strong person can feel weak from fatigue, the nemesis of everyone with MS. Increased endurance will also help you minimize and deal with those bouts of fatigue.

Flexibility increases your movement capabilities, which may help you gain better control of your body. Control certainly enhances your confidence during the problem days, but it also makes you feel good about your body all the time, something everyone hopes for.

The cardiorespiratory component is an obvious necessity for anyone's good health and fitness. It is even more important for a person with a medical problem. You do not need other complications in your life.

All these physical fitness components are features of exercise through HYDROROBICS. And with "hydro" you will eliminate the negative aspects of other forms of exercise that are especially harmful to you.

You can exercise in water without getting overheated! You must *not* get overheated! Sam Wright urges us to "stress water temperature" as a critical factor in a water exercise program.

The Red Cross Aquatic Therapy Handbook recommends 80 to 84 degrees as the appropriate water temperature for persons with MS. We caution you to remember that you will get warmer as you exercise, especially as you do the aerobic exercises of HYDROROBICS. It's really better to begin your exercise session in water that feels cool, but not cold. If the water feels warm when you enter the pool, it's probably too warm for exercise. Use good judgement about this—in addition to weakness, you are also risking fatigue.

Which leads us to the other dangerous potential side effect of most forms of exercise. No one understands the difference between "tired" and "fatigued" the way a person with MS understands it. Your life is constantly complicated with decisions of balancing activity versus the risk of fatigue.

We especially wanted Dr. Wright's opinion regarding exercise versus fatigue. You are exercising to be fit—and to prevent inactivity from allowing your muscles to stiffen—but when is inactivity more important than exercise? His advice? "Your body gives you the signal. Exercise just up to the fatigue level—but no more."

Someone we know very well was even more specific on this question of when to stop—and, in some cases, of when to avoid completely. Kate had been doing a HYDROROBICS program of exercise before she was diagnosed as having the benign form of MS, over three years ago. She was so pleased with the benefits of "hydro" for physical fitness and for her appearance that she never considered halting her exercise routine.

"But I was never really sure when I needed complete rest more than I needed the exercise. Some days, it would just be so much easier to never leave the nearest chair. Even when I knew I'd feel better after my time in the pool, I couldn't get up enough energy to get there. I really felt guilty about that."

Dr. Wright suggests that Kate learn how to pace her activity. And he recommends two ways that Kate, and you, can do this more easily.

1. Pick the time of day when you feel the best as your exercise time, and
2. Allow yourself breaks if you need them; pace your exercises.
    But he urges you to "stay active."

HYDROROBICS can easily fit into Sam Wright's suggestions. If you don't have the energy for one-hour vigorous workouts 3 times a week, pick your time of day and have shorter, vigorous workouts more often. And if there is no way to predict when you will feel your best, because MS is rarely consistent in how or when it affects you, change your exercise habits as you need to, in the same way you've learned to make changes in the rest of your life.

"Hydro" is easy to stay with because it's adaptable to your needs. You are in control of how you use it. But remember Dr. Sam Wright's advice, "Stay active."

References

Orthopedic Section

Duffield, M.H. *Exercise in Water*. Baltimore: The Williams and Wilkins Company, 1969.

Kuprian, Werner (ed.); Eitner, Doris; Meissner, Lutz; and Ork, Helmut. *Physical Therapy of Sport*. Philadelphia: W. B. Saunders Company, 1981.

Cardiac Section

Magder, Sheldon; Lennarrson, Dag; and Gullstrand, Lennart. *The Effect of Swimming on Patients with Ischemic Heart Disease*. Stockholm, Sweden; Karolinska Institute, 1981.

National Heart, Lung and Blood Institute. *Exercise and Your Heart*. Washington, D.C.: U. S. Department of Health and Human Services, 1981.

Stress Section

Gottlieb, William. "Your Emotions and Your Health: A Woman's Guide." *Spring*. April 1983.

Vitale, Frank. *Individualized Fitness Programs*. Englewood Cliffs, N.J.: Prentice-Hall, Inc., 1973.

Wilson, Ira H., and Kasch, Fred W. "Swimming As a Clinical Tool." *J.A.P.M.R.* May-June, 1967.

Arthritis Section

Arthritis Foundation. *Arthritis: The Basic Facts*. Atlanta: Arthritis Foundation, 1978.

Arthritis Foundation. *Home Exercises for Arthritis Patients*. Atlanta: Arthritis Foundation, 1974.

Multiple Sclerosis Section

Bauer, Helmut J. *A Manual on Multiple Sclerosis*. International Federation of Multiple Sclerosis Societies, 1977.

Guenther, John R. *But You Look So Well*. Chicago: Nelson Hall, 1978.

Ottenberg, Miriam. *The Pursuit of Hope*. New York: Rawson Wade Publishers, Inc., 1978.

RX-Therapeutic Claims in Multiple Sclerosis, under the auspices of the International Federation of Multiple Sclerosis Societies, 1982.

Consultants

Cardiac Section

John D. Cantwell, M.D., Cardiology
Preventive Medicine Institute
Georgia Baptist Medical Center
Atlanta, Georgia

Stress Section

Phillip W. Wierson, Ph.D.
Director, Counseling Center
Georgia State University

Multiple Sclerosis Section

Sam Wright, M.D.
Physical Medicine & Rehabilitation
Emory University
Outpatient Director
Shepherd Spinal Clinic
Atlanta, Georgia

14

INJURY: YOU DON'T HAVE TO GIVE UP EXERCISE!

No one likes to be injured. Besides the possibility of losing time on the job (and that means money), you may have to temporarily give up your favorite recreational sport or physical fitness activity. Then, too, there's the pain and discomfort. Ugh!

Well, if you're like most people, you'll want to get back to a normal lifestyle as soon as possible. In order to facilitate rehabilitation of your injury, your physician may have advised you to engage in mild exercise. Although you might prefer to continue your regular exercise such as tennis, racquetball, jogging, etc., you may find that the activity aggravates your injury. This will be particularly true of an injury to the lower body. So, what do you do? For a possible answer, let's consider a friend of ours, Jeff Whalen, who was faced with the same dilemma.

Jeff, a businessman and enthusiastic road runner who is frequently seen in Atlanta racing circles, suffered a broken foot at age 33. After preliminary medical treatment, his doctor gave him the traditional bad news that accompanies injuries of this type—six weeks in a cast, and six months of limited activity. In fact, Jeff's physician recommended that he give up running altogether because, in Jeff's case, running was damaging the bones in his feet.

That advice was hard for Jeff to swallow. Was this the end of his exercise career? All his dedication to the sport and now this! "There doesn't seem to be any justice in the world," Jeff thought. People run to improve their cardiorespiratory fitness, but then face a 'trade off' between developing a good cardiorespiratory system and causing potential damage to the bones and joints of the lower body.

Well, Jeff wasn't the type of person to quit exercising that easily. The benefits of physical activity were too important to him. He instead chose a HYDROROBICS exercise program recommended to him by a friend.

Jeff religiously performed the exercises during his six month recuperation period and was really impressed with his new form of exercise. Of course, he took it easy at first, then increased the intensity of his exercise as his foot got stronger. In addition to gaining normal use of his foot faster than predicted, he discovered that HYDROROBICS helped him not only maintain, but improve his overall level of physical fitness.

Jeff may have broken his foot, but in the healing process he discovered a new and exciting form of exercise which he has permanently added to his regular exercise routine. He learned that with HYDROROBICS you can achieve the necessary cardiorespiratory benefits—*without* any "trade-offs."

HYDROROBICS in Perspective

HYDROROBICS was the answer for Jeff, and it might be the same answer for you. Many people in similar situations have found HYDROROBICS to be beneficial because:

- you can maintain or improve your overall physical fitness;
- the physical characteristics of water can make it *easier* for a person with an injury to exercise; and
- the water's therapeutic qualities may aid in the healing process.

Although we mention that HYDROROBICS may have a therapeutic effect, we are in no way claiming that HYDROROBICS is a treatment in itself for the rehabilitation of injuries. We are only suggesting that it may be a *supplement* to medically advised treatment in a nonclinical setting. This view is supported by the many physicians we have consulted. They also emphasized that, because there are so many different types and degrees of injuries, it would be best to discuss the possible limitations of exercise with your physician or physical therapist. By working with these medical professionals, you can modify the HYDROROBICS exercises to accomodate both the development of your total physical fitness and the rehabilitation of an injury.

HYDROROBICS *Supplements* the Rehabilitation Process

Now that you have everything in perspective, you are probably curious about how exercising in water can supplement the rehabilitation process. If you read about "HYDROROBICS Defined," you learned that several physical properties of water play an important role in the development of physical fitness. These same physical properties also provide us with answers to the rehabilitation question. The primary properties to consider are buoyancy, resistance, pressure and temperature.

Buoyancy is the one physical property we should all be thankful for; it helps make exercise in the water more pleasurable than painful. Remember Archimedes' Principle? In simple terms, it means that the weight of a body submerged in water is reduced by 90%. If you weigh 120 pounds on land, you will weigh only 12 pounds fully submerged in water. By the way, this is as close as you'll get to the weightlessness astronauts experience in space.

Buoyancy allows you to move more easily by minimizing the constraints of gravity you encounter on land. Compression of weight-bearing joints in the spine and legs can occur while exercising on land, but is virtually eliminated while you are in water. Think of how many joggers you know who repeatedly complain of muscle strains, ligament sprains, joint pain, even possible stress fracture from the continuous pounding of their feet on pavement. Maybe this is why some runners look as if they're having a miserable time.

As you move your limbs through water, the *resistance* of the water against the moving body parts helps create an overload for the muscles performing the movements. The amount of overload can be varied in two ways. First, the speed of the exercise movement can be varied such that, the faster the movement is performed, the greater the resistance to your body part moving through the water, and the greater the overload to the muscles promoting the movement. Second, the amount of overload can be increased by adding objects to the moving limbs. This increases the difficulty of moving the limb through the water. For example, use "flippers" on your feet while you attempt to perform a kicking motion underwater.

Thus, if you have an injury that has caused pain and weakness to a joint and surrounding areas, you can perform exercises underwater, controlling the overload so it easily accomodates your functional ability and available range of motion. This helps minimize atrophy of the supportive muscle tissue while helping maintain available joint function. As your injury slowly heals, you will be able to gradually increase the methods of overload. Eventually, your muscles will regain their full functional strength.

Water *pressure* works in harmony with the water's resistance to help create an overload, but an overload that primarily affects the circulatory and respiratory systems instead of your skeletal muscles. As soon as you submerge your body in water, the heart, blood vessels and lungs are subjected to an increase of pressure from the water which demands increase in their activity.

One goal of the rehabilitation process may be to increase blood flow to the injured area. But beware! Since many injuries are accompanied by swelling and pain, your physician will probably advise you to apply cold applications to the injured area during the first few days. Limiting blood flow to your injury will help keep the swelling and pain to a minimum. After the first few days, you may be advised to perform light exercise in order to increase blood flow. Remember, if you have an injury and you're not quite sure how to treat it, *be on the safe side and consult your physician*!

The last physical property is water *temperature*. Why do we leave this one for last when it's the first thing you react to upon entering the water? Because, let's face it, unless you own a heat-regulated pool, there is not much you can do to control the water temperature. The important implication here is that warm water tends to dilate your blood vessels and increase blood flow, while cooler temperatures constrict blood vessels and slow down blood flow.

This too can help in the rehabilitation process. But again, you must take precautions about stimulating blood flow to an injured area *too soon*. Also, realize that warm water tends to relax your muscles. If you add the massage effect that moving water has on your body, there's a chance you could (under the right conditions) fall asleep in the water. This is one reason hot tubs can be dangerous.

Most public and private pools try to keep an ideal temperature, somewhere between 78-84 degrees F. It is generally preferred to have the water slightly cooler, since the body's movements will create heat, helping you adjust to the water temperature. However, if you don't move a lot, or participate in a low-key exercise routine (e.g., early stages of an injury), you will probably feel more comfortable in warmer water (82-84 degrees F).

Now that you better understand the relationship between water exercise and its therapeutic qualities, you know that it isn't necessary to give up exercise just because you're injured. But remember, there are many different types and degrees of injuries, and it's best to consult a physician before you jump in the water and do HYDROROBICS.

HYDROROBICS and Specific Injuries

Too often, people self-diagnose their injury and prescribe treatment and exercise for themselves. The danger in self-diagnosis is that you may make the wrong decisions about treatment and exercises, resulting in further damage to the injured part of the body. If you follow proper precautions, your chances of maintaining or improving your overall total physical fitness and speeding up the healing of your injury will be good.

Whether you have decided on your own or have been advised by your doctor to exercise, the following general information may help you as you begin your HYDROROBICS program with an injury.

There are several types of common injuries—or minor injuries—which may be helped by a "hydro" exercise program. Some examples of minor injuries are first and possibly second degree muscle strains and ligament sprains, mild forms of bursitis, and punctures and lacerations of the skin. These are the types of injuries people tend to treat by themselves. Possible symptoms are mild pain, inflammation and partial loss of function of the affected body parts. Except in the case of punctures and lacerations, where you must keep the affected area dry, you probably can do some HYDROROBICS. You may have to limit your activity at first but, with the proper selection of exercises, you can continue to maintain or improve your general physical fitness. Keep in mind you might have to alter the suggested "hydro" fitness levels to accomodate your injury.

More serious injuries such as chronic back problems, extreme injuries from accidents, severe musculoskeletal problems, or a complex postoperative condition, e.g., corrective surgery, will definitely require the supervision of a medical specialist or physical therapist when beginning an exercise program. Serious injuries usually involve a recovery period followed by a lengthy recuperation period. For example, if you had an orthopedic problem, you may be required to wear a cast for a six or eight week period. During this time you won't be able to enter the water, but you may be able to perform some special land exercises (isometric, isotonic, isokinetic) as prescribed by your physician or physical therapist. Such exercises help prevent muscles from atrophying. Once the cast is removed, your doctor may let you perform some light exercises in the water in order to restore strength to the injured area and improve your range of motion.

Several physicians and physical therapists we've spoken with are very much in favor of their patients using HYDROROBICS during a rehabilitation period. This is primarily because the minimum weight environment created by water helps decrease the possibility of reinjury to the affected body part(s).

Also rated highly was the exerciser's ability to control the amount of force applied to the injured limb while moving through water. It is possible to move a limb in the water through the available range of motion while slowing down the movement, thus decreasing the overload where pain persists. This self-protecting mechanism helps prevent reinjury while allowing muscle development and improvement of joint function.

Precautions

Although the physicians and therapists support use of water exercises during a rehabilitation period, they also pointed out some general precautions you should follow.

First, give special attention to symptoms of pain, inflammation, and the extent of loss of function of the injured body part. If these symptoms increase in degree or persist for more than a week, consult your physician immediately. In other words, if your injury is either *staying the same or getting worse* during your first few exercise workouts, you'd better see a physician.

Second, approach your first few workouts cautiously—do not overwork your injured part(s). Exercise in short bouts and give yourself enough time to rest between exercises. Let the healing process take its normal course. Remember, it's better to "underdo" than "overdo" exercise at this time.

Third, you may have been advised to use cold applications on your injury the first few days. During this time you may be asked not to exercise the injured area and to stay out of the warm water of a pool, especially in the summer. Besides, you'll probably just want to rest the first couple of days—any injury can send trauma throughout your whole body. So "go with the flow" and don't be too anxious.

Fourth, if you are on medication, especially painkillers, you may want to delay any exercise. Medication distorts the body's ability to monitor the pain mechanism, and you might apply too much force to your injured area without knowing it, causing greater damage.

Fifth, if you had a cast removed, take it easy at first because of the weakened muscles. Most orthopedists suggest you exercise with moderation for the first two weeks. Just aim at moving the injured limb as much as possible through its full range of motion in the water. After two weeks, you can begin to apply force, increasing it as you begin to restore full use of the limb. In the case of surgery, it's important to let the affected area heal fully before you enter the water in order to prevent infections.

"Let's look at how some of the things we've mentioned applied to one person with a serious injury, Linda Garner.

An auto accident left Linda with fractures of the leg and hip and a long recuperation period that included physical therapy. Although her hip was shattered, the joint socket was not damaged, and she thought she should be making more progress than she was.

When Linda informed her orthopedist that she was beginning HYDROROBICS on her own, he cautioned her not to overdo, and at first she continued the physical therapy. She felt good in water but was very tired after each early "hydro" session. After a few weeks, however, Linda was so impressed with her increased flexibility and muscle tone that she added extra workouts.

What does Linda think of HYDROROBICS for someone with an injury? "I recommend it to people I meet with any injuries—hand, arms, legs—and older people who have flexibility problems." Both her doctor and Linda are impressed with her degree of recovery. But she also *enjoys* water exercise. "It's fun. It's the best exercise."

Linda Garner got back into exercise and speeded her recovery at the same time. The bonus was that she had a good time doing it!

Can you still remember the title of this chapter? If not, go ahead and look—we'll wait. We're hoping that after reading the chapter you'll agree with us: just because you are injured or had an operation, you don't have to stop exercising. Remember Jeff Whalen? Jeff was really "down in the dumps" when he learned he couldn't run because of his injury. When he discovered HYDROROBICS, he was thrilled because he could continue to maintain his physical fitness.

So, if you've recently been injured, why don't you discusss the HYDROROBICS program with your physician? If your physician encourages you to start a program, then you, like Linda and Jeff, may discover a very pleasing and exciting new form of exercise. When your injury finally heals, and you decide to return to your regular acitivity, we won't be offended. But we're betting you'll want to continue with your HYDROROBICS exercise program. We think it's that good! Happy exercising.

References

Eriksson, B., and Furberg, B. (editors); Nelson, C., and Morehouse, C.A. (series editors). "Proceedings of the Fourth International Congress on Swimming Medicine." *International Series on Sport Sciences*. Vol 6. Baltimore: University Park Press, 1978.

Kuprian, W. (ed.); Eitner, D.; Meissner, L.; and Ork, H. *Physical Therapy of Sport*. Philadelphia: W. B. Saunders Company, 1981.

Reilly, Thomas (ed.). *Sports Fitness and Sports Inquiries*. London and Boston: Faber and Faber, 1981.

The American College of Sports Medicine; The American Orthopaedic
Society for Sports Medicine; and Sports Medicine Committee of the
United States Tennis Association. *Sports Injuries—an Aid to Prevention and Treatment*. Connecticut: Funded by Bristol Myers Company.

Consultants

Jenny Evans
Physical Therapist
Emory University

Peter J. Harmeling
Athletic Trainer
Georgia State University

Gary S. Sutton, M.S., R.P. T., A.T.C.
Sportsmedicine Clinic
Atlanta, Georgia

Joseph S. Wilkes, M.D.
Orthopedic Surgeon
Piedmont Hospital
Atlanta, Georgia

15

AGING: DISCOVERING THE FOUNTAIN OF YOUTH

Nothing's right if you don't feel good.—June Drew, age 61.

Please don't think we're trying to be clever when we say this, but some of the youngest people we know are the older people who practice HYDROROBICS.

These are the same people who *continue* to exercise with "hydro," who believe they have discovered something wonderful, something they wish they had known about sooner. We can call it a "Fountain of Youth"—or "pool of youth," if you like. Whatever it's called, it works very well for a large number of people.

Some you met in other chapters for reasons other than age. A few were attracted to "hydro" because of medical problems, some because they were concerned about cardiorespiratory fitness, others because they are weight conscious or found that other forms of exercise increase the chance of injury.

In fact, older people do HYDROROBICS for all the same reasons younger people do. It's just that they are aware of additional reasons for exercising that younger people sometimes don't think about.

As you get older, your body does change, but it doesn't have to change drastically. You can exert some control over those changes! More and more people in their 50's, 60's and 70's are discovering this.

B. J. Clark was 54 years old when she first took a course in HYDROROBICS. "Within a month of starting (the course) my endurance and stamina were increasing rapidly. I can now get through my normal workday without that midafternoon slump. That's a great feeling, believe me."

It's been more than two years since B.J. began HYDROROBICS, and she has continued with it for a variety of reasons; she has firmed up, dropped a size in clothes, and improved her flexibility. B.J. suffers from bursitis, tendonitis and arthritis, but she suffers a lot less now because of HYDROROBICS. She looks slim; she moves like a much younger woman. She *feels* like a much younger woman!

You can probably relate to at least some of the reasons B.J. chose HYDROROBICS as her form of exercise. Three of her physical problems have become less bothersome. She has improved her appearance, improved her energy level, and feels more youthful as a result.

B.J. is still quite young. What about some people in their 60's?

June and Lawrence Drew were in their 60's when they tried HYDROROBICS. Like so many other married couples, one of them wanted to do something and the other partner joined in to keep him company.

Lawrence was overweight, found that running bothered his legs, but knew he needed exercise. June's reason was, " 'Cause my husband wanted to take it." They both benefitted more than they had hoped for.

"It improved my wind and my physical condition. If you do 'hydro' with tight muscles, they'll be limber before long—you'll feel better," Lawrence offered.

June "just did it for fun," and because of her husband. "It has helped me to limber up a lot. I feel relaxed (something a lot of people say after HYDROROBICS), and I have better flexibility."

One benefit of exercising as a couple became obvious from seeing them together. They were doing something for themselves as individuals, but they were doing it as partners. The *companionship* of exercising was part of the fun. (Those who play together, stay together!)

You may want to encourage a husband, wife, other relative or friend, regardless of their age, to join you in your new HYDROROBICS program. Remember, HYDROROBICS is designed for a variety of fitness levels. You can enjoy working out with your partner while each of you exercises at your own level. You can work at a different level, at a different speed or pace from your partner, with the results that are right for you.

As you *gradually* build up your strength and endurance, your fitness level may progress to the next stage. But don't be disappointed if it doesn't happen too quickly. The important thing is that you have started to exercise.

Okay, you say. That may be fine for B.J. Clark or June and Lawrence Drew, but not for me. Why not? Your age is not a factor in whether to begin exercising! Remember, you have all the same reasons as anyone at any age, and more.

Your doctor can probably give you a number of reasons why you, specifically, should exercise. And, of course, you will be getting a medical checkup before beginning an exercise routine. That will be a good time to get advice on any special limitations you might have because of a medical condition.

If there are no health problems, your limitations will probably be the ones you set for yourself. Rather than setting limitations, why don't you set some goals? It is a waste to set an arbitrary limit for a healthy body when exercise helps keep you in that healthy condition and can improve it!

Just Healthy?

It's impossible to say that all the people at a given age are alike and need to do the same things. At any age, even your age, you may be both healthy and physically fit. If you're not sure of the difference, remember that to be *healthy* means to be free of disease or infirmity and well nourished. The President's Council on Physical Fitness and Sports calls it "organic fitness." To be *physically fit*, what the Council calls "dynamic fitness," includes the efficiency of heart and lungs, muscular strength and endurance, balance, flexibility, coordination and agility.

If you are both healthy and physically fit, exercise can help you stay that way, and chances are you already include some sort of regular exercise in your life. We think you'll like HYDROROBICS as your method of exercise.

If you are healthy but not fit, you have a head start over a lot of other people, regardless of age. It means you don't have any special considerations caused by a medical condition. It means you are in the best possible condition to begin a gradual program of increased activity. It must be gradual if you have not been active at all. If you are currently performing some form of exercise (perhaps vigorous walking, swimming, or maybe tennis two or three times a week), you should have no trouble adding HYDROROBICS to your plan. We suspect you probably are not active, though (or you'd be fit as well as healthy), so you'll want to personalize your exercise program at one of the lower fitness levels. You can always move up a level when you get used to exercising and have increased your strength and endurance.

"I wish I'd known about it lots longer. I feel really good," is the way Gladys Nuggles (age 55) put it. It is never too late for a healthy person to increase his or her fitness level, and you may take extra pleasure in looking and feeling younger than your years.

Without Pain

Gladys does have a health problem—arthritis. Be sure to read the chapter on health problems if *you* have some specific health needs. But remember, you don't have to have health problems just because you are getting older! Although your body changes with age, you have some control over those changes. You don't have to accept them as a given factor in your life.

For most people, health—good or bad—is not a given. We all have friends or family members who have health problems and continue to do the same unhealthy things responsible for those problems. Yet, they are in control. They have *chosen* to do those things. They could just as easily have chosen to do the opposite—to be weight conscious, to stop smoking, to limit the amount of alcohol they drink, and to make exercise a part of their lives.

Whether you have a problem and want to make some changes, or are healthy and want to stay that way, you too can be in control. As June Drew has told us, "Nothing's right if you don't feel good." People who practice HYDROROBICS, at *any* age, tell us that they feel good because of it.

We're not saying HYDROROBICS or any other water exercise program will replace any medical treatment or therapy you need for your specific problem. We are saying a physically fit person is more likely to be a healthy person. You body will be in a better condition to fight off disease, and age has nothing to do with this!

But what about the problems we tend to associate with aging? According to Raymond Harris, M.D., in "Leisure Time and Exercise Activities for the Elderly" (from a book published by the American Medical Association), "Proper exercise can delay or at least retard changes associated with age in the musculoskeletal, respiratory, cardiovascular and central nervous systems."

Dr. Harris lists four basic elements in an exercise for older people: "(1) relaxation, (2) exercise of the endurance type to condi-

A physically fit person is more likely to be a healthy person.

tion the heart, lungs and circulation, (3) muscle-strengthening exercises, and (4) stretching exercises to improve joint mobility and reduce the aches and pains accompanying the aging process."

We would make one adjustment to that statement—the aches and ,pains that *may*, but do not have to, accompany the aging process. HYDROROBICS fits all four of the criteria, and is performed in the comfort of water with all its therapeutic effects.

Water exercise gets special treatment in *The Fitness Challenge . . . in the Later Years* (an exercise program for older Americans), published by the Administration on Aging. The section "Swimming and Water Exercises" opens by describing an exercise regimen in water as ". . . such a good activity it deserves special mention," and goes on to point out that water makes it easier to do some exercises (buoyancy) while causing resistance for certain other exercises.

This booklet, written in conjunction with the President's Council on Physical Fitness and Sports, also recommends swimming and water exercises for people who have feet or leg problems. You may not be a swimmer, and you don't have to know how to swim in order to do HYDROROBICS. But, much research has been done on the health of participants   in the Master's Swimming program. The oldest swimmers to have competed in these swimming meets for older persons were 88 and 91. As a group, the Master's Swimmers tend to have lower blood pressures than the mean for their age in the general population. For more on the Master's Swimmers, read "Master's Swimming Program Stimulates Fitness Motivation" by A. J. Arthur in *The Physician and Sportsmedicine*, October, 1976.

Something in addition to improved physical health and fitness happens when people such as the Master's Swimmers get together. It's the kind of companionship that we observed in June and Lawrence Drew. Exercising with others can keep your emotional life vital and encourage a positive mental outlook. The "buddy system" is also an excellent way to prevent missing a workout.

If you do have your own home swimming pool, you may want to invite others over to try HYDROROBICS with you. Or you can certainly check out the nearest "Y", community college or university pool. Many of these facilities might even give public courses on HYDROROBICS.

These are good ways to make new friends and boost the relationships you already have. Every source we've consulted on water exercise for older people emphasizes this very approach.

HYDROROBICS was designed as an individual activity. But it can be anything *you* want it to be at any level that you need it to be—at any age *you* happen to be.

References

Administration on Aging and the President's Council on Physical Fitness and Sports. *The Fitness Challenge . . . in the Later Years.* Washington, D.C.: U. S. Government Printing Office, 1968.

Arthur, A. J. "Master's Swimming Program Stimulates Fitness Motivation." *The Physician and Sportsmedicine* October 1976.

Harris, Raymond. "Leisure Time and Exercise Activities for the Elderly." *The Humanistic and Mental Health Aspects of Sports, Exercise and Recreation.* Edited by Timothy Craig. Chicago: American Medical Association, 1976.

Jamieson, R. H. *Exercises for the Elderly.* Emerson Books, Inc., 1982.

Consultant

Frank Whittington, Ph.D.
Department of Sociology
Georgia State University

HYDROROBICS, as a total physical fitness program, can help athletes prepare for sports competition.

16

ATHLETE: IMPROVING YOUR SPORTS PERFORMANCE

We thought this topic should be included because we have met so many serious recreational and "week-end" athletes interested in improving their sports performances. In addition to taking lessons to improve their technical skills, these athletes eventually realize that developing their physical fitness or sports conditioning is just as important. Several people have told us that they initially selected a recreational sport like tennis, racquetball, etc., as a way to enjoy themselves and to improve their physical fitness. However, after a time they became "wrapped up" in the sport and very competitive. Sometimes their competitive interests overtook their physical fitness interests.

HYDROROBICS, as a total physical fitness program, can help athletes prepare for sports competition, but it is not in itself a complete training program. Before we discuss how HYDROROBICS can help you in your sport, let's consider some basic concepts of sports performance.

Specificity of Training

Training athletes to improve their performance is a complex matter. You do not develop abundant strength and expect that this alone will make you successful in your sport. Frank I. Katch and William D. McArdle, in their book *Nutrition, Weight Control, and Exercise*, discuss the principle of specificity of strength rather delicately. They state that, "The correct application of force in relatively complex, learned movements, such as the tennis serve or the shot-put, depends on a series of coordinated neuromuscular patterns, and not just the strength of the muscle groups recruited during the movement . . . Consequently, strengthening muscles for use in a specific activity such as golf, rowing, swimming, or football requires more than just identifying and overloading muscles involved in the movement. It requires that training be specific with regard to the exact movements involved."

In other words, tennis players wanting to develop more strength in their forehand swing should overload the tennis racquet and practice the swing motion repeatedly.

In their book, *Sports Conditioning and Weight Training*, William J. Stone and William A. Kroll state that, "Specificity means that the sports skills are highly unique; that no matter how much 'alike' they appear, there are usually a number of minor differences that make it difficult to perform many skills well without a great deal of practice. Furthermore, one cannot carry over athletic performance from one sport to another unless the two are nearly identical."

Have you ever switched from tennis to golf or racquet ball to softball and realized how uncoordinated you felt in the second sport? Not only that—do you remember how sore you got? Muscle soreness exemplifies how specificity of training works. Even though you use the same muscles, you are using them differently. Stress factors are applied to the muscle and tendons at different angles which can have varying degrees of strain.

If you're thinking about taking up a new sport or are seasonally changing sports, you should begin a specific physical conditioning program to help you adjust to this new sport's demands. HYDRORO-BICS will help with some sports like tennis, golf, baseball, etc, where you can make particular movements from the sport underwater.

Effects of Strength Training

We all know you can increase your strength by repeatedly overloading the muscle. What many of us don't realize is that, in addition to the muscle growing in size (hypertrophy) due to an   increase in the size of the muscle fibers, the nerve pathways between the brain and the muscle develop simultaneously. According to Stone and Kroll, "these nerve or motor pathways become so vigorously bombarded with messages from the brain that the efficiency of this traveling system is greatly improved in strength training. The implication here is that as you learn the skill and mechanics of the strength building exercise, efficiency of the movement in the exercise results in more effective use of force."

That is why, if you apply the theory of specificity of training in your strength training program, you will have a better opportunity to improve a particular skill in your sport.

Skill-Related Fitness Components

Developing a sport skill can take a long time, and the degree of improvement will vary from person to person. There is a wide variety of sport-related fitness components that must be developed, such as speed, power, coordination, balance, agility, and reaction time. Additionally, performance is affected by the degree and balance of our emotional and mental well-being on a given day. Therefore, you can appreciate the complexities that a coach must deal with in the training process—especially with a high performance athlete like an   Olympian.

Because Joe works with the U.S. Olympic Committee, he has been able to observe the sophisticated Olympic sports medicine training program on site at the U.S. Olympic Training Center in Colorado Springs. There, potential Olympic athletes are subjected to a rigorous testing regimen which includes physical fitness evaluation, biomechanical and kinesiological analysis of sports performance, sports physiology and more. As a result, each athlete's coach is given a detailed analysis of that athlete's capabilities and the design of a customized training program to help the athlete fully develop his potential in that sport.

Whew . . .! We bet you can begin to feel the pressures an Olympic athlete must go through on the way to making an Olympic team and possibly winning a gold medal. Realize though, that you're just an ordinary weekend athlete and don't have the privilege of an elaborate sports medicine training program. But, if you're willing to try HY-DROROBICS, we will show you how to begin developing the strength and power aspects of your sport skill. First, we will identify several recreational sports and suggest a HYDROROBICS training program for each; second, we'll discuss how "hydro" may help you if you have a sport-related injury.

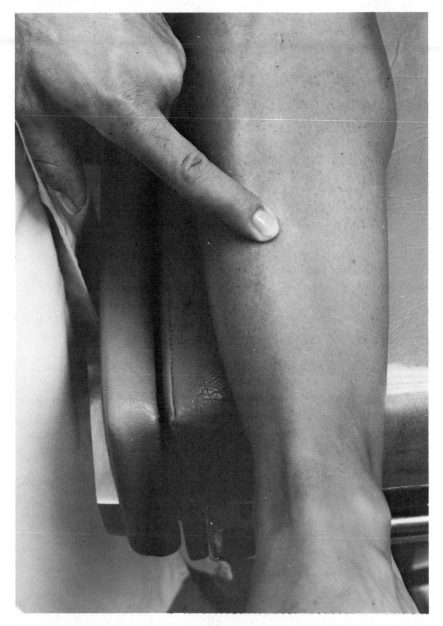

HYDROROBICS may help you if you have a sport-related injury.

HYDROROBICS Conditioning for Sports

Our basic approach in using HYDROROBICS as a conditioning program for specific sports is as follows:
- Design a total fitness program developing all the components of physical fitness.
- Select and emphasize special "hydro" exercises that will help you develop the specific and supporting muscles involved in the skill.
- Practice the specific skill in the water (with equipment, e.g. tennis racquet, baseball bat, etc.) according to the specificity of training principle.

In order to design a total physical fitness program, consult the chapter, "Designing Your Personalized Program." Select the appropriate suggested "hydro" program that appears in the Appendix according to your fitness level.

Once you have your basic "hydro" progam identified, you can supplement it with the following suggested "hydro" exercises, which will help improve your overall sports performance.

Tennis and Racquetball

Specific Exercise:

With an old tennis racquet, position yourself in chest-deep water in the basic tennis-ready position. Perform the normal back swing and them either the complete forehand or backhand stroke. Remember to step forward as you stroke and follow through with the swing. Return to the starting position. Repeat several times until you begin to tire. You might vary your approach by doing 8-10 repetitions, slowly concentrating on form and a smooth stroke. Then perform 8-10 maximum strength repetitions. This may be repeated depending on your fitness level.

General Exercises:

Hands, arms and shoulders:
- Tidal Wave
- Arm Circles
- Mae West
- Wing Flap
- Wrist Action
- Agitator

Torso:
- Body Twist
- Six Count Twister
- Universal

Legs:
- Ankle Action
- Calf Builder
- Pendulum
- Lateral Lift
- Flamingo

Golf

Specific Exercise:

With an old golf club or other similar object, stand in shoulder-depth water with your ready stance. Perform the backswing to the water's level and then execute the full golf swing again to the water's level. You won't be able to complete the full swing because you want to stay under the water for its effect. Also, try not to hit the bottom of the pool during the swing. Repeat as suggested in the section on tennis and racquetball.

General Exercises:

Hands, arms and shoulders:
- Tidal Wave
- Arm Circles
- Golf Swing
- Figure 8
- Double Arm Lift and Press
- Finger Flow
- Agitator

Torso:
- Six Count Twister
- Body Twist
- Hip Dip
- Universal

Legs:
- Scissors Cross
- Plié
- Lateral Lifts
- Calf Builder

Softball and Baseball

Specific Exercise:

Take an old softball or baseball bat and stand in shoulder-depth water with the batter's stance. Swing the bat through the complete swinging motion. Repeat as suggested in the tennis and racquetball section.

General Exercises:

Hands, arms and shoulders:
- Wrist Action
- Finger Flow
- Agitator
- Traffic Cop
- Arm Pendulum
- Shoulder Shrug
- Figure 8
- Mae West
- Arm Circles

Torso:
- Six Count Twister
- Double Leg Lifts
- Body Twist
- Hip Dip
- Universal

Other Sports

Many other sports or specific events, e.g., track and field, and running sports like soccer, etc., can take advantage of water exercises in the training program. Using the few sports listed above as examples will enable you to adapt the basic "hydro" program into a personalized training program for your sport.

Sport-Related Injuries

Sport injuries are quite common in both recreational and competitive sports. We all dread injury because it means temporarily discontinuing play, not to mention all the inconveniences that go along with an injury.

There is a difference between injuries suffered by an ordinary person and those of an athlete. While the rehabilitation process for an ordinary person usually ends when they can perform normal daily activity, an athlete's rehabilitation must continue to a higher level of activity and be designed to meet the specific demands of that athlete's sport. That is why knowledgeable recreational and professional athletes refuse to be treated by a family doctor when they have a serious injury; they prefer to be treated by physicians who specialize in a new medical field called "Sports Medicine." These physicians have both expertise in basic medicine and specialized training in a wide variety of sports-related sciences such as exercise physiology, biomechanics, kinesiology, etc. They are also extremely knowledgeable about the demands of athletics.

We should also mention the importance of an athletic trainer. Although trainers are not physicians, they are important in prevention and rehabilitation of athletic injuries. They can assist the athlete in designing strength and flexibility training programs, and prepare the athlete for competition. With the use of such techniques as taping, external heat and cold applications, massage, etc., an athlete can compete in forceful activity with minimum chance of injury. If injury occurs, the athlete may be able to continue play after the trainer administers these techniques.

If you are an athlete, we hope you will try HYDROROBICS as a way to develop your sports performance. We feel that HYDROROBICS is a winner, and that might help make you a WINNER!

References

Katch, Frank I., and McArdle, William D. *Nutrition, Weight Control, and Exercise*. Boston: Houghton Mifflin Co., 1977.

Stone, William J., and Kroll, William A. *Sports Conditioning and Weight Training*. Boston: Allyn and Bacon, Inc., 1978.

17

SEXY: THAT'S RIGHT—SEXY!

This chapter is dedicated to all the beautiful, sexy people we know who have given a special meaning to HYDROROBICS. They are packaged in various shapes and sizes. Some are young, but many have lived a good number of years. They first tried "hydro" for a variety of reasons, but they all have achieved something exciting in the process of attaining the original goal.

Roger strides out to the pool with a look of confidence. Rita glides along with an aura of self-satisfaction. B.J. approaches exercise with the excitement of a much younger woman. They all have something wonderful in common; they epitomize the sexuality of people who are physically fit, who feel good about themselves, who know they look as good as they can. They are sexy!

Now, let's get back to you. Everyone can and should be sexy. You are entitled to being and feeling sexy for as long as you'd like. Part of it is mental attitude, part of it is the way you look (but *only* a part), and a great deal of it is the totality of you as a healthy and fit human being. Looking like Robert Redford or Sophia Loren would be a waste if you didn't have the energy or vitality that goes with being attractive and sexy.

No one can define what being sexy means for you. Fortunately for all of us, there are as many definitions of who is sexy as there are people expressing such opinions. But if we can't give a blanket list of *who* is sexy that will please everyone, we can certainly share a pretty certain list of *what* is sexy. We're even more sure about what is *not* sexy! That our list has agreat deal to do with HYDROROBICS should come as no surprise to you.

Not Sexy

Flab is not sexy. But a firm body with the right muscle tone looks good no matter what shape it's covering. As you tone your muscles, using HYDROROBICS, you will also notice a loss of inches, in places that need to lose, and the overall effect of a trimmer you. Other people will notice too. That's sexy.

People who tire easily, don't have much energy and don't have the strength to enjoy life's pleasures are not sexy. But a person who has developed a strong cardiorespiratory system and has the stamina to enjoy recreation as well as work, who has the glow often called "vitality," is going to be an enjoyable companion, no matter what the pastime. That's sexy.

A person who slouches and stoops, lets the body sag where it will and doesn't walk with pride is not sexy at all. But the people we mentioned earlier—Roger with his self-confidence, Rita with her satisfied look, and B.J. with her zest for living exemplify what you can give yourself through HYDROROBICS. The total effect is definitely sexy.

Let's get explicit, without getting X-rated (sorry, folks—not this book). You already know that the improvements in your appearance through HYDROROBICS will add to your self-image. They add good things to both what you think about yourself and to what you project to others. Your feelings about yourself are sending messages to others that this is a very special person, the kind of person we'd all like to know better.

So what's behind those messages? What is the person that you are projecting really like? Are you healthy? Have you dealt with stress in a beneficial way? Are you physically fit? Do your heart and lungs have the capacity to enjoy a healthy sexual relationship? Have you strengthened the muscles of your body so that they can respond and reciprocate to the pleasure of physical activity with another healthy human being?

You'll notice we haven't mentioned perfection of any kind. We don't care if your nose is crooked or your breasts aren't the ideal size or you're too short or too tall or not enough whatever. They'll be the first to admit it, but the people we've told you about do not have perfect beauty. Sexy isn't perfect.

Sexy Hormones

Several studies done independently on Olympic athletes and on runners at Emory University in Atlanta show that exercise increases the level of testosterone, a hormone that affects sexual desire, in both men and women.

Of course we already know that people who exercise feel better about their bodies, and people who feel better about their bodies are more comfortable with their own sexuality. What's more, you should be able to feel sexy for as long as you'd like to feel sexy. Older people who take good care of their health and physical fitness are more likely to continue enjoying the benefits of a fit body for as long as they wish.

And according to Edwin Dale of Emory University's School of Medicine, women who exercise regularly usually have fewer problems connected with menopause. Everything seems to get better with exercise.

Back to HYDROROBICS

Now that you've met some sexy people and learned about sex and exercise, let's look again at "hydro" and sex. One physical fitness component we haven't talked about is flexibility. A limber body can do all sorts of interesting things that enhance a sexual experience.

If you'd like to concentrate on exercises to increase your flexibility, look for the word "stretch," especially for the "static stretch" or hold position. Also, at the top of each exercise, most-affected body parts are indicated. Check these. You'll want a total approach to fitness for your body, but don't hesitate to emphasize the exercises for those body parts you think need special attention.

We personally think that such exercises as the *Flamingo*, which includes a static stretch and works the thighs and groin area, is a good example of a "sexy" exercise.

The *Leap Frog* combines both endurance and a very sexy leg position that can increase flexibility. Experiment with your own choice of exercises to find out what can be sexy for you.

Our last advice to make the most of being sexy through HYDROROBICS should be obvious. Invite someone to try "hydro" with you. It could be someone you know well or someone you'd like to know better. But it most certainly will be someone who won't mind the results. We'll leave that selection up to you.

We know you'll both enjoy HYDROROBICS.

References

Lowe, Carl; and Nechas, James. "Shape up Your Sex Life." *Spring*, May 1983.

PART FOUR

HOW TO STAY WITH IT!

18

HOW TO STAY
WITH IT!

If you're the type of reader who reads the last part of a book first, keep reading. What we're going to tell you in this chapter is that HYDROROBICS is the kind of physical fitness program you can stay with and will enjoy staying with.

You'll certainly want to work your way back through the chapters and read some of the comments made by people who already enjoy "hydro" and its many benefits. In doing so, you'll discover that HYDROROBICS is an exercise program for almost everyone, probably you.

The important part we've saved for last. It deals with something critical to the success of any exercise efforts, even a fun program like HYDROROBICS. You must stay with it!

We'd like to suggest a few ways to make it easier, but none of them work without your efforts. You can begin before you ever get into the pool, by talking your way into HYDROROBICS.

Talking HYDROROBICS

Tell your family, close friends, anyone who knows you well enough to encourage you, that you are going to begin exercising. If you're thinking you'd prefer to keep all this quiet, just until you decide if you want to stay with it, we think that you ought to try our way instead. Here's why.

One of the best forms of motivation we know of is the encouragement and support from the people close to us. If they care about you, they will be pleased at your efforts and will tell you so. Besides, it won't be easy to keep your progress a secret for very long; the changes are hard to conceal from those who know you well.

There may be gradual weight change, and if this is your goal there will be an accompanying eating change. You'll not only want family and friends to notice, you'll want their support for your efforts. Having moral support does not minimize the importance of what you are doing for yourself. It does allow those close to you to share a little of that importance.

Two's Company—and So Is Three

Now that you've told everyone about your exercise plans, why don't you ask one or two of those people to join you? Besides the fun of exercising with someone, you'll appreciate the mutual support to continue a regular program. It is not as easy to skip an exercise session when you know that someone else is counting on you to be there. Your "hydro" partners may be reluctant to join you at first, but your pleasure in the program will probably encourage them to give it a try. Be sure to point out to them that they can individualize their exercise routine to their own fitness levels and still work out with you.

The Beat Goes On

Whether you're on your own or with others for your HYDROROBICS routine, the addition of music can make exercising a more exciting experience. A portable radio or tape recorder with lively dance music will give you a tempo to work with and will keep you moving. The aerobic exercises are especially suited to musical accompaniment. But all the "hydro" exericises seem more like fun when there's a beat to follow. Planning your music for specific exercises can also add to the enjoyment. Or you may want to call a local radio station and request certain songs or types of music for the time that you regularly work out. The radio announcer will probably appreciate your consistent listening.

Creatures of Habit

You may not have noticed, but in the last paragraph we referred to your "regular" routine. It's very important for you to begin thinking of exercise as a regular part of your routine—right now.

Pick the best time of day for you to exercise, perhaps when you have the most energy, or the most time, or just when you need an exercise pick-me-up the most. Now, stick to that time.

You may want to plan a weekly schedule that includes exercise with your professional and personal activities. Be realistic, but make a workable plan and stay with that plan. We *are* creatures of habit. This is one habit that may last a lifetime.

Results and More Results

What will probably keep you with your HYDROROBICS program more than anything is the results you will achieve. After about 6-8 weeks of "hydro" workouts, you should experience some very tangible results.

You will certainly notice a new sense of well-being that goes along with regular exercise. Others will notice too. You will be more relaxed, and you will have more energy. Yes, the two are possible at the same time.

But, if you have been exercising three times a week for about an hour, and if you have really been putting some effort into your exercise workouts, you will also be seeing some measurable results. Even if you do not need to lose weight, your muscles should be toning up, and that means a change in measurements.

Do you think you can stick with something that is fun to do for about 6-8 weeks in order to have a trimmer waist, or thighs, or whatever needs to be trimmer?

Do you think you can stay with it even longer — for more results? This is where it gets even easier. Can you handle 10 weeks? 12 weeks? More? It'll get easier to stay with HYDROROBICS because you *will* see more results as you continue.

People Talk Back

All those people we asked you to talk to in the beginning should be talking back to you. They will be telling you how great you look and how proud they are of you. They might also be asking you to tell them about HYDROROBICS again, if they didn't really listen the first time. This time they may want to join you. Don't forget to give them the support that they gave you when you needed it most.

Your Biggest Fan

No, we don't mean your doctor, although hopefully you have shared the good news with the physician in your life. More than likely, you've gotten lots of encouragement to exercise for the sake of your health and overall physical fitness.

The fan who can help you most is the one who has the most knowledge of what it really takes for you to exercise. The person who most appreciates what you are doing is *you*, the one doing it. Go ahead and tell yourself how wonderful you are. Being wonderful consists of feeling wonderful and looking wonderful. If that doesn't make you want to stay with HYDROROBICS, we don't know what will.

Maybe you have chosen to exercise for a spouse or other relative, or to look more attractive, or because of a health condition (or to prevent one), but all the reasons still fall into one category. You are doing this for you. And you will stay with it for you.

The compliments are nice. In fact, as your weight stabilizes to the ideal for you, the compliments will be more than nice. But compliments just reinforce what you already know as you incorporate HYDRORO-BICS into your life.

"Hydro" will be what you want it to be for you. It can be the fun way to maintain your weight without special dieting. It can be the means to strength and flexibility for your muscles. It can be the best way to achieve physical fitness when you have some medical condition or temporary health problem. It can be the way to reduce stress.

We can only reinforce what Lawrence Drew (see Chapter 15) says about "hydro." "I have found that what you get out of it is directly proportional to what you put into it." This is an exercise program you can stay with and will want to stay with. Congratulations on choosing HYDROROBICS.

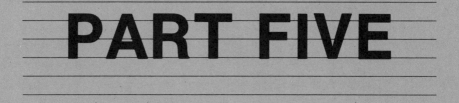

PART FIVE

APPENDICES

A

FITNESS PROFILE FORM

DATE OF TEST _____

I. Physical Fitness Test

A. Cardiorespiratory—Step Test

	Men	Women	Point Value
Above Average	119 or under	125 or under	3
Average	120 to 149	126 to 154	2
Below Average	over 150	over 155	1
		Points Earned	_____

B. Flexibility— Bend and Reach

	Men	Women	Point Value
Above Average	+ 4.5″ or over	+ 5.5″ or over	3
Average	+ 1″ to + 4″	+ 1″ to + 5″	2
Below Average	0″ and below	0″ or below	1
		Points Earned	_____

C. Muscular Strength and Endurance

	Men	Women	Point Value
Above Average	46 or above	40 or above	3
Average	30 to 45	25 to 39	2
Below Average	29 or below	24 and below	1
		Points Earned	_____

D. Body Composition

	Men and Women	Point Value
Above Average	Below 1″	3
Average	1″	2
Below Average	Over 1½″	1
	Points Earned	_____
	TOTAL FITNESS SCORE	_____
	(Add all the points	
	earned in each test)	

II. Determining Your HYDROROBICS Fitness Level
Determine your fitness level by finding the range for your Total Fitness Score.

		Check
Above Average	(10-12 pts.) Fitness Level A	_____
Average	(7-9 pts.) Fitness Level B	_____
Below Average	(4-6 pts.) Fitness Level C	_____

III. Establishing Specific Fitness Goals
   A. Determine which of the following specific fitness goals interest you.
      1. Body Contouring
         a. Arms
         b. Waist
         c. Hips
         d. Thighs
         e. Legs
      2. Weight Loss
      3. Improving Sports Performance
         a. Golf Swing
         b. Tennis Swing
         c. Racquetball Swing
         d. Baseball Swing
         e. Softball Swing
   B. Refer to Appendix C and select the workout for your fitness level. For *body contouring,* select the part of the body (lower, mid, upper) you want to develop and concentrate your time interval in this area. You will also have to pick the specific HYDROROBICS exercises that affect that body part. For *weight loss,* you simply need to emphasize the aerobic exercises in your program. For improving sports performance, consult Chapter 16.

IV. Calculating Your Training Pulse
   You'll need this for your aerobic workout.

   226 (men use 220) minus age $= A$ _____.
   A _____ minus resting pulse rate $= B$ _____.
   B _____ $\times$ 60% $= C$ _____.
   B _____ $\times$ 85% $= D$ _____.
   C _____ + resting pulse rate $= E$ _____ .
   D _____ + resting pulse rate $= F$ _____.

NOTE:
- To find your resting pulse, take your pulse in the morning before you get out of bed.
- A and B represent your training pulse range. If you're just beginning an exercise program, use the 60% (E) training pulse rate.

B

LIST OF HYDROROBICS EXERCISES

Aerobic

Bunny Hop
Charleston
Charleston Flap
Cheerleader Jump
Chorus Line
Cossack Shuffle
Cross Country Skier
Downhiller
Flutter Kick
Gerbil Wheel
Heel Slap
High Jump
Joggernaut
Jumping Jacks
One Leg Hop
Polaris
Scissors Jump
Side Leg Side

Lower Body

Ankle Action
Calf Builder
Flamingo
Half Moon
Lateral Lift
Left-Right-Left
Leg Circles
Leg Stretch
Pendulum
Plié
Quad Stretch
Scissors Cross
Swift Kick
Wide Leg Kick

Middle Body

Body Twist
Double Leg Lift
Fire Hydrant
Hip Dip
Hula Hoop
Leap Frog
Modified Scissors Cross
Six Count Twister
Windshield Wiper

Upper Body

Agitator
Arm Circles
Arm Pendulum
Double Arm Lift & Press
Figure 8
Figurehead
Golf Swing
Mae West
Quack, Quack
Shake
Shoulder Shrug
Tidal Wave
Traffic Cop
Wing Flap
Wrist Action

Potpourri

Devices
Inner Tube Laps-Arms
Inner Tube Laps-Legs
Universal
Water Treading

C

Sample HYDROROBICS Workouts

Fitness Level A
(Total Workout = 60 minutes)

Warm Up Period	(5 minutes)
Aerobic Exercises	(30 minutes)
Body Exercises	(20 minutes)
(lower, mid, upper body)	
Cool Down Period	(5 minutes)

Fitness Level B
(Total Workout = 50 minutes)

Warm Up Period	(5 minutes)
Aerobic Exercises	(20 minutes)
Body Exercises	(20 minutes)
Cool Down Period	(5 minutes)

Fitness Level C
(Total Workout = 40 minutes)

Warm Up Period	(5 minutes)
Aerobic Exercises	(12 minutes)
Body Exercises	(18 minutes)
Cool Down Period	(5 minutes)

D

PROPER WEIGHT REDUCTION TECHNIQUE

Calculate Ideal Body Weight

        Males: 106 lbs. plus 6 lbs. for each additional inch over 5 feet.

        Females: 100 lbs. plus 5 lbs. for each additional inch over 5 feet.

        Then: Subtract 10% for small frame.
                 No change for medium frame.
                 Add 10% for large frame.
                 Ideal Weight: _____ lbs.

Calculate Caloric Needs

    Basal Metabolism-Caloric Needs

        Ideal Body weight $\times$ 10 KCal/lb

                = _____ Basal Calories.

Sedentary Person-Caloric Needs

        Basal Calories + 20% = _____ Calories.

Moderately Active Person

        Basal Calories + 40% = _____ Calories.

Very Active Person

        Basal Calories + 70% = _____ Calories.

Weight Reduction Formula

    Decrease caloric intake + Increase physical activity = (−) Energy balance. (A decrease of 3500 calories is approximately equal to the loss of 1 lb. of fat.)

    *Never take in fewer than 1200 calories per day—you will not get the necessary nutrients.

SAMPLE 1200 CALORIE DIET

16 oz. skim milk	160 Kcal
4 oz. lean meat, low fat cheese, eggs	300 Kcal
3 servings vegetables (raw or steamed)	85 Kcal
3 servings fruit (fresh or water packed)	225 Kcal
4 servings whole grain bread, cereals	280 Kcal
3 oz. margarine, butter, salad oil	150 Kcal
Total Intake	1200 Kcal

E

GLOSSARY (Understanding the Language of HYDROROBICS)

aerobic capacity	the maximum amount of oxygen the body can process within a given time
aerobic(s)	exercises that increase heart and lung activity to the extent that additional oxygen is required (from *New Aerobics* by Ken Cooper)
blood pressure	the pressure of the blood in the arteries. Can be positively affected by the amount of exercise you perform
body composition	percentage of fat contained in the human body
body contouring	the process by which muscle tone is improved in specific areas of the body leading to a reduction in girth measurement
*cadence	the measure or beat of movement (see speed)
calorie	unit used to express food energy
cardiac	pertaining to the heart
cardiorespiratory	pertaining to the heart and lungs
cholesterol	a fatty-like substance found in the blood stream which has been linked to coronary heart disease
circulatory	pertaining to the heart, blood vessels, and blood circulation
*dip	the action of lowering a portion of the body in the water
*duration	length of time to perform an individual exercise
electrocardiogram	(ECG, EKG) a graphic record of the electric currents produced by the heart as used by a physician or physiologist to measure heart response to exercise
*fitness level	used here to describe your personal physical fitness level as determined by the HYDROROBICS physical finess test
*flex	to bend or contract
flexibilty	one of the major components of physical fitness defined as the degree of range of motion of a limb which can be improved through HYDROROBICS

*Indicates a term used in one or more of the HYDROROBICS exercises.

*forceful	movement with greater speed and determination (with total commitment)
*frequency	the number of repetitions
genetically disposed	the tendency to have something occur because of genetic design
*gutter rail	channel used to draw off excessive water at side of pool. In HYDROROBICS, used for upper body stabilization
**HYDROROBICS	read the book!
hydrotherapy	medical use of water to treat certain physical disorders
isokinetic	a way of contracting a muscle by moving a body part through its full range of motion with a fixed weight and constant speed of movement
isometric	contracting a muscle in a fixed position for a specified period of time
isotonic	contracting a muscle during the full range of motion of a limb against a fixed resistance
*lateral	to the side
maximum oxygen uptake or Max VO2	the amount of oxygen processed by the body during exercise
muscle group	the primary and secondary muscles used in moving a body part
muscle toning	the process of tightening your skeletal muscles through exercise
muscular endurance	the capacity or quality of the human body to endure physical work over specific periods of time or large numbers of repetitions of movement. A major component of physical fitness
muscular strength	the ability of the muscle to lift the maximum amount of weight in one repetition. One of the major components of physical fitness
overload principle	the process of subjecting a muscle to a greater workload until it adapts to increased demand
physical therapy	treatment of a disease and injury by mechanical means (exercise, heat, light, massage, etc.)
*prone	lying with the front or face downward
*repetitions	the number of times you repeat a complete exercise
*stabilizing	making resistant to sudden change or condition
*static stretch	prolonged holding of a specific stretch position
*supine	lying on the back, having the face upward
training pulse	the working pulse rate at which the body positively benefits from exercise

*Indicates a term used in one or more of the HYDROROBICS exercises.